Abusing Memory

The Healing Theology of Agnes Sanford

JANE GUMPRECHT, M.D.

Canon Press
MOSCOW, IDAHO

Jane Gumprecht, *Abusing Memory: The Healing Theology of Agnes Sanford*

© 1997 by Jane Gumprecht.
Published by Canon Press, P.O. Box 8741, Moscow, ID 83843

01 00 99 98 97   7 6 5 4 3 2 1

Cover design by Paige Atwood Design, Moscow, ID

Printed in the United States of America.

ISBN: 1-885767-27-7

Contents

Introduction

The progression of events which led to the writing of this book began with the realization that the New Thought cult in which I was involved before I became a Christian had teachings similar to the New Age movement, especially in regard to healing. New Thought is the religious arm of the New Age movement.

I was asked to listen to the tape of a seminar given at a Baptist church by a Christian counselor. The morning session was within orthodox Christian boundaries, but in the afternoon, the counselor taught the participants to visualize "Jesus" forgiving the "inner child." This involved relaxation, centering, and controlled breathing, which is the yoga discipline of yoking the mind with Brahman in the Hindu religion. In the West, this is called self-hypnosis.

I thought this lovely, personable Christian counselor must be uninformed or even deceived about her healing session. I prayed for guidance. As a physician and a Christian, I hoped she would listen to my concerns. She was gracious when I went to talk to her, but I was a little taken aback to find her husband was with her. He is head of the department of psychology at a church affiliated college. He did most of the talking; I did not make much progress.

At that time, I knew little about Agnes Sanford, except for what I had learned during my days in the Unity School of Christianity (now called Unity Church). But I had some doubts about her ministry. As I was leaving, I mentioned Agnes

Sanford. In reply, the counselor's husband said, "Agnes is a much maligned saint." I decided to read Agnes Sanford's books to find out what she believed. This book is the result of my reading.

I started by leafing through Agnes's *The Healing Touch of God.* At one point, Agnes writes, "I taught him only the teachings of Jesus Christ, lending him Dr. Emmet Fox's *Sermon on the Mount,* still a standard for this purpose."[1] She also wrote in her autobiography that Fox's book "thrilled my soul"[2] and that she derived her theology of redemption from it. Her admiration for Fox set off the alarms in my mind. Emmet Fox was the preeminent lecturer for the cult Unity. I still have my copy of his book from the time when I was ensnared in New Thought.

Agnes is well-known as the mother of the Inner Healing/Healing of Memories movement. She almost single-handedly brought it out of Jungian psychology and New Thought into the Christian church. She was able to do this because of her impeccable credentials as the daughter of missionaries to China and as the wife of an Episcopalian pastor.

Most inner healing advocates acknowledge their debt to her, and her "theology" is evident in their ministries. John Loren Sandford (no relation to her) dedicated his books to her as his beloved mentor. Morton Kelsey learned healing of memories from her as well. Karen Mains of the Chapel of the Air was trained in inner healing at the School of Pastoral Care founded by Agnes and her husband. Similarly, spiritual therapist Leanne Payne is a disciple of Agnes, as was the late Ruth Carter Stapelton. Glen Clark, who established Camps Furthest Out, published Agnes's first book, *The Healing Light.* Glen Clark's books read like Unity textbooks. *The Healing Light* was also endorsed by Theosophy, the first of the modern New Age cults.

I realized that to understand Inner Healing/Healing of Memories, Christians must understand what Agnes taught since she pioneered the work. For that reason, I am focusing on the writings of Agnes Sanford to explain Inner Healing.

The Bible is Our Standard

Defenders of Inner Healing often claim that their critics are neglecting the good in their work. Their criteria for embracing a program is largely pragmatic—if it works, it's worth utilizing. But we can know if a strategy truly works in the long run, only if it is compatible with biblical doctrine. Saul consulted the witches of Endor even though Deuteronomy 18 forbids it. It seemed to work, in the short term. Saul received the answer he had vainly sought from God. But 1 Chronicles 10:13 makes it clear, God didn't condone an occult way of determining "His will," even though it "worked." Saul paid with his life.

God's Word is truth, and so we need to examine the basic theological foundation of Agnes Sanford's beliefs. If she taught things contrary to biblical doctrine, we must throw out the teaching, whether it appears to work or not. In the past, the name of these teachings was heresy. Throughout history, men have paid with their lives to defend God's Word against the very heretical doctrines that are accepted today by many who take the name of Christ.

Agnes was a loving and multi-talented woman, who believed God had given her a very important mission in life. I am sure she thought she was a Christian because of her heritage, marriage, knowledge, and mystical experience. My intent is not to demean her as a person. Rather, I write this book in loving concern for my brothers and sisters in Christ. I ask you to consider prayerfully the evidence presented herein. Read Agnes Sanford's books for yourself and then evaluate the Inner Healing/Healing of Memories movement. Jude 3 and 4 commands Christians to "earnestly contend for the faith" and to be wary of those who have "crept in unawares" into our churches and "deny the only Lord God, and our Lord Jesus Christ." John tells us, "Beloved, do not believe every spirit, but test the spirits to see whether they be of God; because many false prophets have gone into the world." (1 John 4:1).

Basic to the evaluation of a person's Christian belief is an examination of their concept of God, Jesus, and the Holy

Spirit. This is the foundation. All cults start with unbiblical beliefs about God, and their other errors develop out of these misconceptions. The Inner Healing movement grew out of Agnes Sanford's mental image of God, so this is the first area that I will explore in this book, after some biographical sketches. Some other subjects will be:

• Her inner rebellion toward the orthodox church.

• Her struggle with the "why of suffering" and God's will, and its impact on her decision to develop a healing ministry.

• Her meaning of "a prayer of faith," "prayer from a distance," and "intercessory prayer."

• Her claim to have had a direct commission from God and had human mentors like New Age leader Emmet Fox.

• Her view of Jesus traveling through time today to do inner healing.

• Healing of Memories in light of the second commandment.

• Origins of the Inner Child concept and biblical teachings concerning the Inner Child.

• Her concept of the unconscious.

• Her frequent use of popular New Age terms.

Chapter One:

Mother of Inner Healing

Controversy continues to swirl around the memory of Agnes Sanford's life and work in the few years since her death in 1983. Was she a much-maligned saint? Was her theology biblical? Did she revitalize dead orthodoxy? Were her teachings disguised New Thought?

These questions deserve an answer in light of the increasing acceptance of Inner Healing by Christians in evangelical churches, and especially because so many Christian couselors and pastors use her Healing of Memories techniques.

The foundation determines the soundness of the superstructure. Without a firm foundation walls crack, bridges collapse, skyscrapers fall. Our spiritual well being relies on a biblical foundation that will withstand stress. We expect physical foundations to crumble eventually, but the foundation of our life must be eternally sound. Christian devotees of Inner Healing are building on the foundation laid by Agnes Sanford.

Children attending Sunday School learn the story Jesus taught about the man who built his house upon a rock in contrast to the man who built on sand and the dire consequences of his foolishness (Matt 7; Luke 6). Scripture gives us clear direction: "I laid a foundation and another man is building upon it. Let each man take care how he builds upon it. For no other foundation can anyone lay than that which is laid, which is Jesus Christ" (1 Cor. 3:10-11, RSV).

Jesus Christ must be the only foundation for the Christian life. Flawed foundations can be camouflaged. Therefore, it will be of primary importance to see if the foundation of Inner Healing and Healing of Memories is biblical in view of its incredible claim to being as important to the Church as the Reformation.

Biographical Background

Her death leaves us with her beliefs as reflected in her writings. The preponderance of this book will be devoted to an in depth examination of her own recorded words, with only a brief discussion of the facts about her life. I'll start with a brief look at her life as gleaned from her autobiography, *Sealed Orders.*

Agnes White Sanford was born in 1897 into a distinguished Virginia family. Her ancestors included several professors at Washington and Lee University as well as Stonewall Jackson's chaplain. Her father, Hugh Watt White, was a southern Presbyterian minister and missionary to China. She spent her formative years in the Chinese towns of Hsuchoufu, Yencheng, and Shanghai.

She was sent back to the United States at age 14 to attend Peace Institute, a small Presbyterian school for young ladies. She lived in the United States during World War I and spent her final school years studying at Agnes Scott College in Decatur, Georgia.

Demonstrating her independent spirit, she gave up a B.A. degree so she could bypass "subjects I did not like: higher mathematics and science and French"[1] which were required for a degree and opted instead for "fascinating courses in short story writing and the science of poetry and the theory of beauty."[2] While in college she wrote, "I hungered to know all that I could learn about the stars and nebulae and all the company of heaven. Was I not one of them? We all entered into an expanded awareness of the universe that has been of tremendous value in my expanded awareness of God."[3]

Sanford had determined at age twelve that she would

not be a missionary, yet she had no real home except in China, so she returned to China. Later she taught at St. Mary's School in Shanghai, and then in Soochow Academy, an Episcopal school for boys, where she met her future husband, who ran a boy's school in the nearby town of Changshu.

Ted Sanford was a shy, young, Episcopal priest, nine years older than Agnes, whose "Chinese was so atrocious, he would never be appointed as a minister of a Chinese church,"[4] according to his bishop. Ted and Agnes married April 3, 1923. Thirteen months later she gave birth to a son. That summer Agnes had one of the bouts of depression which intermittently marked her life.

In 1925, they were furloughed home to Media, Pennsylvania. Resigned to always being a teacher in China, Ted began taking courses in education in Philadelphia with the goal of receiving an M.A. degree. Throughout all of this, Ted's secret desire was to be a minister of a church so he accepted with alacrity the call to be pastor of the Episcopal Church in Morristown, NJ. This was to the dismay of his wife, who would never again see her beloved China. Agnes had been looking forward to returning to China where her only duty would be that of a minister's wife:

> The kind of person I used to be was dead. And the new person I was forced to be had much trouble in living. My work was to care for husband, children and house. That was made clear to me. Therefore, I closed the doors of my mind to childish notions of writing or creating beauty in drama or paint, and set myself to do my whole duty as wife and mother. . . . So I delighted in my little ones and longed for another. But underneath the domestic joys, there was always the feeling that the real me was dead.[5]

Agnes also made it clear that, although she loved her husband, they had difficulties in their marriage relationship. Her novel, *Lost Shepherd*, is a thinly disguised story of Ted's resistance to her religious theories and his eventual, reluctant acceptance of them. She admitted that she fell in love more than once but "never thought of breaking the bond of marriage, even though it was founded more on spiritual values than physical ones."[6]

After the birth of her third child, depression began to descend upon her once again. When Jack was eighteen months old she ascribed this "darkness of depression" to various "wounds" she had suffered. The wounds were disaffection with marriage, a longing for China, and nightmares over horrors she had seen in China. But "the basic trouble was that I had forgotten whence I came, and I did not know the sealed orders with which I had been sent to this earth."[7] She contemplated suicide.

This was the pivotal time of her life. Through a minister who laid his hands on her head and prayed a "prayer of faith" she felt instantly "healed" of her depression, although depression dogged her footsteps periodically until she died. This exciting, emotional experience made her sing and shout all the way home and also caused her to begin to search for the reason for her healing. Her Inner Healing theory was the eventual result.

The remainder of her life was devoted to spreading the good news of the gospel of healing. She described this as a "driving compulsion" which consumed all her talents for writing and speaking. She began with a Bible class for young mothers and gradually developed a national ministry through her School of Spiritual Healing. "We renamed" it "The School of Pastoral Care as being a less alarming name for clergy to contemplate."[8] For a long time her husband viewed her religious ideas with great skepticism but gradually began to accept them and even worked with her in establishing the School of Pastoral Care. After the death of her husband, she continued faithful to her "sealed orders" which she felt she had been called by God to obey. The last decade of her life she slipped into senility and probably Alzheimer's syndrome.

In subsequent chapters we will examine why and how she developed her theology of the Inner Healing.

Chapter Two:

A Free Spirit

From an early age, Agnes Sanford was in total inner rebellion against the orthodox teaching of her missionary parents and the southern Presbyterian Church. Later, she showed a similar rebellion against the Episcopal Church, though she was married to an Episcopalian minister. With her family she studied the Bible from Genesis to Revelation over and over again. One summer, she sat in Sunday school with "eyes glazed with utter boredom."[1] She preferred to read Dickens and Scott, rather than the "holy books of the Sunday school."[2]

She developed a "certain cynicism concerning piousness, which lasts to this day."[3] Yet she loved the hymns, the view from the windows, and her friends. She also loved the sermon when attending worship services for "I had long ago taught myself to turn off my mind when wearied of a sermon and tell myself a story."[4] She gave no hint in her writings that her parents were legalistic in their daily living, and she seemed to love them dearly. Even so, she believed there was something wrong with Christianity. "I was not at all sure that the Episcopal Church was sound. But then I had never been sure that the Presbyterian Church was sufficient for life—for joy—for something I could not express."[5] This questioning of the reality of God began with fears and troubles that seemed to overwhelm her.

Sanford recounted in her autobiography the most troublesome fear "that I have ever known." It entered her

life when she was seven. Her father had a nervous breakdown, and she began to fear that he would die. Two years
later her world crumbled and fell apart when the other missionaries had a bitter disagreement with her father who wanted
to give the Chinese ministers more freedom and authority in
the Chinese church. She lost faith in the missionaries who now
appeared as her father's enemies: "I lost faith also in God.
For these people were 'completely Christ-centered and Bible-
centered' as they love to say. Their God was real, and Jesus
was their loving Savior. Therefore, Somebody Up There
should have been able to help them."[6]

Over fifty years after this episode, Sanford wrote of it in
a manner which demonstrated her continuing disenchantment
with Christ-centered and Bible-centered Christianity: "From
the very beginning until now I prefer deeds to words and I
am not delighted by the saccharine smiles of those who bear
down upon me to report a 'mountaintop experience' concerning some 'precious soul.'"[7] This attitude of cynicism, indeed, tended to spread to Christianity in general.

Other problems invaded her world when her baby sister, who had survived diphtheria and measles, died from
amoebic dysentery. Loneliness was added to her burdens when
Isabel, her dearest friend, was sent off to school in Shanghai.
"It might be expected that in my loneliness I turned to the
Lord. No, I didn't. I was rather fed up with the Lord, if the
truth must be told."[8]

Perhaps the reason she could not turn to the Lord is because, prior to the death of her baby sister, she had gone into
a Buddhist temple and while there, she wondered if "these
idols have some power after all? What would happen if I
myself were to worship the great Buddha?" She folded her
hands and bowed before the "serene gilded idol" and mur-
mured "O-me-to-fu" as the monks did. "Nothing happened.
Or did it? I wonder. For gradually there came to be within
me another voice, sneering, despising, scorning me."[9] Perhaps she opened herself up to a malignant spirit, especially
since she wrote in her first book years after this episode, when
she was "healed" of depression,

Readers may wonder whether my real trouble may have been demon possession. It occurred to me long afterward that this may have been one of the troubling factors. I remember the time as a child I had worshipped the huge brass Buddha to see what would happen, thus opening my mind to a power that was not God, as one does when playing with a Ouija board or with automatic writing.[10]

Later during her healing ministry years she recorded, "At this point Satan entered me, and I began to wonder whether it was God's will for him [Ted Sanford's friend] to die."[11] This is not a frivolous statement. The Bible records that Satan entered Judas. But I don't believe Satan can enter into Christians for they are all indwelt by the Holy Spirit of God (Rom. 5:5; 8:9; 1 Cor. 2:12; 6:19-20; 2 Cor. 5:5). Satan can deceive, discourage, and fool a Christian, but he cannot dwell where the Holy Spirit dwells, as indicated by 1 John 4:4, "Greater is he that is in you, than he that is in the world."

Recently I had a conversation with Pastor John L. Sandford who was Sanford's "mentor as well as my pupil, my spiritual father as well as my spiritual son."[12] He told me that he exorcised oppressive spirits from her in 1962 or 1963. This was when Agnes had been in the ministry for over ten years.

In her extensive writings and in her autobiography she made ambiguous statements about her relationship to Jesus and Satan. She wrote in her autobiography that she had been converted at the age of nine, that she remembered "the gentle Southern Presbyterian minister who made sure of my salvation," and that the experience moved her to tears.

On the other hand, eight pages later, she looked back at her childhood and said,

> I marvel again at the goodness of God who has returned to me a thousandfold all the beauty for which my starved heart yearned in childhood. I did not know Him then. I had heard with the hearing of the ears, and I had given my heart in love as best I knew how to His Son Jesus Christ, but I did not know Him.[13]

Sanford "entered into eternity" in her thirties when she and Ted were on vacation in a cottage by Warren's Pond in New Hampshire. There beside the "dancing waters of the lake I prayed that God's life would enter into me through the sunlight. It happened. In a time that was not time, I was beyond time—I was filled with unbearable bliss—from this time forth I knew God."[14] Considering God's life to be sunlight is pantheistic.

She wrote about the aftereffects of this experience as puzzling and frightening for she had an intense burning within her head like a live coal and a tightness around her head like a tight band. Twice after this time she had similar experiences of receiving light and the "Light-giver" when she "opened the door by asking for it."

These were all experiences and in none of them is there any mention of acknowledgement of sin or the need of a Saviour who had paid the penalty for her sin to reconcile her to God. In fact, she wrote,

> For many years I had been the channel through whom others might receive healing. I knew that this healing included forgiveness—that is the healing of the personality—the changing of the emotional tenor. . . . I had thought a great deal about forgiving others, but I had never thought of being forgiven because I was not in the least conscious of sin.[15]

Not only was she not conscious of sin, but she had an unbiblical concept of forgiveness. To her, forgiveness was the "healing of the personality, the changing of the emotional tenor." However, as 1 John 1:9 says, "if we confess our sins, He is faithful and just to forgive us our sins and cleanse us from all unrighteousness." We see, then, that sin in the biblical sense is falling short of the righteousness of God. Sin is not an emotional or personality problem. Forgiveness is predicated on our recognition that we sin—an apparent problem with Sanford.

Sanford had so many confusing and ambiguous "conversion" experiences and encounters with Satan, it leads us to one of two conclusions; she was never sure of her salvation, or she was not saved. Only God knows. Once, when writing to others she said, "But there is one trouble with being born and brought up in the church and that is that we may not know whether we ever of our own volition accepted Christ or not."[16]

I had a similar story. My mother had a chronic health problem, so she bagan to seek healing through Christian Science, even though she was a Christian. She was a nurse and became uncomfortable with not being allowed to see a doctor. So when I was in the fourth grade my mother and father began to study New Thought as Unity School of Christianity taught it. My family continued to attend the Presbyterian church and we went to Unity services on Thursday night.

I knew Jesus died on the cross and considered Him divine, because Unity teaches that we are all a part of the Divine mind and Jesus was the perfect example of this truth. But I used to wonder about the "conversion experiences" I read of that some people seemed to have. I decided that because I had always believed there was a God and I attended a Church, conversion was a gradual process as we become more spiritual or had a higher conciousness. Like Agnes I was never certain. Then at the age of thirty-nine, I finally was convicted of sin and made a personal decision to ask Jesus to save me from my sins. There was never any doubt from that time on as to whether I had "of my own volition accepted Christ or not."

Sanford was a free spirit. Her rebellion against orthodox Christianity led her to rely on personal experience over what God says in His Word. Several times in her books she expressed the thought, "experience comes before theology." With this in mind we should not wonder when she gives several confusing and differing accounts of a possible relationship with Jesus.

Chapter Three:

Motives for Healing

The two reasons Agnes Sanford had for going into the healing ministry permeate her biography. These reasons were: the problem of suffering, an inadequate response from the church, and her personal unhappiness.

Suffering and the Church

As an impressionable child, Sanford viewed much poverty, disease, and death. The killing of unwanted infant girls that marked China at the beginning of the twentieth century stood out strongly in her experiences. In addition, her baby sister and the brother of her best friend died, her father had a nervous breakdown, and she feared for his life: "There in the depths [of my mind] there grew a fear, a very common, very natural, very real—the fear of death."[1] Sanford became disillusioned with Christianity. Four times in her autobiography she cried, "something was wrong."

After her college years, during a Sunday evening prayer meeting, a

> beautiful wife [of a missionary] and mother stood up to give thanks that God had healed her spirit after long darkness. . . . Some months later she hanged herself from her bedroom window after trying to cut her wrists. . . . She did not die for several days, during which time the missionaries

besought her to repent and confess her sins . . . poor dear.

It would have been so easy to heal this lovely lady, even as I long afterward was healed. If only some one of God's ministers had known that he himself was a channel for God's power and had laid hands on her and prayed for the love of Jesus to come into her and lift her out of darkness into His light.[2]

Even as a child she had questioned why her parents didn't believe in healing miracles in this dispensation, for she believed that all Christians should be able to fulfill John 14:12 which says, "Verily, verily I say unto you, he that believeth on me, the works that I do shall he do also; . . ."

She wrote, "From this time forth doubt and cynicism entered into a religious experience that had been very real since my conversion at age nine."[3] Apparently she did not understand that Jesus was speaking only to His disciples during the Last Supper. She did not realize the disciples did fulfill this prophecy after His resurrection. This in no manner negates the fact God does heal today, but the incarnation and resurrection were especially surrounded with special miraculous works.

The ability to do miracles was given by God to establish the authenticity of their apostleship and the authority of God while the canon of Scripture was being completed. Thereafter miracles gradually ceased in the Church because Christians had the Word of God as their rule and guide and the Holy Spirit indwelling them to comfort and teach (John 14:16,17,26; 16:13-15; Matt. 12:38; 1 Cor. 1:22; 13:9,10).

The primary reason Jesus performed miracles was to establish before unbelieving Israel that He was the Messiah. If His primary reason for doing miracles was healing alone, Jesus would have healed all the thousands who flocked to Him, or He would not have been compassionate. Instead, His supreme compassion was to die, suffering the wrath of God in their place and for their sin, that they might have eternal life.

Sanford was highly critical of missionaries because they didn't perform miracles when there was illness or death and resigned themselves to the will of God. Years later she wrote in her autobiography about her missionary father and the death of her sister Virginia,

> If he had only known to give himself as a channel for God's power, laying both hands on the child, praying for her the prayer of command—the miracle working prayer: thank you Lord, for it will be so . . . she could have recovered.[4]

Scoffingly she added,

> To limit one's prayers for those in danger by the pious ejaculation, 'Thy will be done' is merely to evade the responsibility. We can cause His will to be done concerning our own loved ones, if we are willing to . . . be conductors of love into the midst of hate.[5]

In another passage, she said, "But let him say, 'If it be thy will,' for that is like spilling medicine on the floor instead of taking it. . . . For while it is not expedient to say 'If,' it is a good thing to say 'Thy will be done.'"[6] Notice the contradictory statements in these two passages about the use of "Thy will be done." This is typical of Sanford in her books when she made a statement that is acceptable to evangelical Christians and then contradicted it by tortuous, convoluted reasoning that negated what she said previously.

Although it is impossible to quote all the passages from her book which are relevant to the will of God, it is abundantly clear from her writings that she did not trust God's will and therefore His wisdom, foreknowledge, omniscience, or most importantly, His sovereignty. She felt compelled to give commands to God in her prayers instead of acknowledging that He is more intelligent than she. Consider Isaiah 55:8-9: "'For My thoughts are not your thoughts, neither are your ways My ways,' saith the Lord. 'For as the heavens are higher than the earth, so are My ways higher than your ways and My thoughts than your thoughts.'" Romans 11:33-36 also confirms this: "Oh, the depths of the riches both of wisdom

and knowledge of God. How unsearchable are His judg-
ments and unfathomable His ways! For who has known the
mind of the Lord, or who became His counselor?"

Sanford also had little patience with the idea of children
of God being subject to suffering.

> I had been brought up on the concept that a certain amount
> of suffering was not only God's will but probably also a
> special mark of His favor. Mother would cheer me by stories
> of Cousin Betty Penick who was a great sufferer and a great
> saint and all her life endured her migraine headaches and
> complained not. (I conceived an intense dislike of Cousin
> Betty Penick.)[7]

Or listen to her sarcasm,

> But to suffer from migraine headaches and say, 'I am a great
> sufferer, but of course Jesus carried His cross and so must I'
> (with a sigh and fluttering eyelashes as though to say 'what
> a saint I am') this is offering Him, in reality our failure to
> carry His cross.[8]

She believed that if through the centuries the Church had
believed in healing, healers now would be so proficient there
would be no illness at all—a man-made heaven here on earth.
Concerning this, she wrote:

> Moreover, if we had not faltered or compromised in that
> battle against the forces of evil that our Lord told us to
> undertake, it is quite possible that we would have brought
> the day in which no child would remain or be afflicted (Rev-
> elation 21:4).[9]

Sanford came to grips with suffering and God's will only
after she devised her own theology of prayer which she called
the prayer of faith. "But learning faith robbed me of the old
comfort of this inadequate concept of His sufferings." She
went on to explain this "inadequate concept":

In my old concept of Christianity, suffering was no problem. This earth was a vale of tears, I was a pilgrim here, it
was God's will that I suffer until I died, and the sooner the
better.... He wanted to share our sufferings so He suffered
too.[10]

With her rejection of her old beliefs she formulated Inner Healing which included her "prayer of faith" or "prayer
of command." She felt they would eventually bring about
the eradication of suffering. In the chapter on Sanford's prayer
of faith I will show that Unity and Science of Mind and other
New Thought/New Age cults use the same prayers and techniques for healing.

Redemptive Suffering

She further tried to resolve her childhood difficulties by
her unique views of suffering which she called redemptive
suffering. She acknowledged that some suffering, which she
called remedial, "is the pain of illness and the grief of disharmony and failure that we have brought upon ourselves and
that can be resolved by prayer and a changed life."[11] Remedial suffering may also be

the chastening of the Lord, or, in more modern words, it is
the striving of our own inner spirits to tell us that something in our lives or in our bodies or in our circumstances
should be healed or forgiven.[12]

I had never heard of "redemptive suffering" before I
read Sanford's books. It is based on her ideas about the blood
of Jesus and the Garden of Gethsemane which I will discuss
later. Her ideas of redemptive suffering followed five steps.
The paragraphs which follow her steps are my critique:

1. *Jesus' greatest purpose was releasing God's love, by which we are
cleansed.* "And at some time in His walk upon the earth He
must have remembered the greatest purpose for which He

came: the purpose of releasing a flow of God's love especially ordained for the unconscious mind."[13] She then wrote:
"we are cleansed by His redeeming love."[14]

God's motivation was love, but we are redeemed and
cleansed by the blood of Jesus (John 3:16; Rom. 5:9; Eph.
1:7; Rev. 1:5).

2. *Jesus must become part of man's subconscious to achieve redemption of man.* "He could not do this from outside of man." In
the Garden of Gethsemane, "in order to redeem the human
race it was necessary to sink deeper into humanity: to become
part of the subconscious mind of *every* man."[15]

But John 1:12 clearly states that Jesus redeems only those
who receive Him.

3. *Jesus opened the connection between the human subconcious and
the spirit.* "Jesus Christ opened the channel between the subconscious and the spirit. He forged into that clogged channel
like a dredger . . . taking the dirt from the mass subconscious
of the race into Himself, then throwing it away upon the shore
of God's Being where the fire of God's Spirit devoured it."[16]

I challenge anyone to find Scripture to buttress these statements. They must turn, instead, to Jung or Eastern religion to
find these thoughts.

4. *Jesus became evil to open the channel, making redemption possible.* "In the Garden of Gethsemane . . . He delivered that
fatal wound [to the serpent's head] by becoming part of evil
that He might destroy evil. In that human living, His heart is
ever open to our sorrows, ever hurt by our neglect and in-
gratitude, ever laboring under our sins. When will we set Him
free so that His Kingdom may be established and His glory
may cover the earth? We can set Him free not only by coming to Him ourselves . . . but also help lead others to
Gethsemane. . . . This is helping Him carry His Cross."[17]

Jesus did not become evil, but sin was imputed to him in
a judicial transaction just as righteousness is imputed to those
who believe in the finished work of Jesus on the cross. Jesus
is not "ever laboring under our sins" for He paid the penalty
once for all for our sins (Rom. 6:10; Heb. 7:27; 9:26). Instead,

He is our High Priest and Advocate who pleads our case on our behalf in heaven when we sin as believers (Heb. 9:24; 1 John 2:1). Therefore, we do not set Him free; God is sovereign.

5. *Every time we sacrifice voluntarily, or suffer, we aid Jesus.* "Every voluntary sacrifice that we make for the purpose of conveying God's love to mankind is helping to carry His cross."[18]

We are "joint heirs with Christ; if so be that we suffer with Him, that we may also be glorified together" (Rom. 8:17). Our suffering does not redeem us or another person; suffering is for sanctification. We also need to keep in mind that the cross is an instrument of death. We take up our cross by putting to death our sins through repentance and confession and then following Jesus.

This flawed theory of redemptive suffering gave some comfort to Sanford who had been very distressed by her childhood experiences and even more by her ongoing warfare with deep depression. In the process of rejecting her Presbyterian heritage, searching for the reason for her trials and for a healing from her depression, she forged a new path—her unusual ideas about Scripture. In her books she makes it plain that she went her own way:

> From the very beginning until now, I prefer deeds to words. . . . I made a decision in those early days from which I never wavered: I would not go all of my life in the bondage of treading only a known path. . . . I would go through untrodden country toward the goal of my choice. . . . I 'laid on the table' all my preconceived ideas and paid no attention to anyone except Jesus—not the Bible nor St. Paul nor my husband nor anyone.[19]

A primary rule for exegesis is not to read into Scripture our own thoughts and prejudices but to take out of the Bible the clear meaning of the words, except for figurative uses. When she said in several of her books that she discarded all Scripture but those concerning Jesus, she revealed a major mistake. If all we needed to know was the four Gospels, why did God give us the rest of the Bible? The Old Testament helps us understand the New Testament which is essential for living the Christian life. After she had already formulated her theology of healing, she did write one book about some of the major persons in the Old Testament but used them to promote her own message. Her criteria for truth was "Does it work?" It was not "what does the Word of God say?" She wrote, "Religion is an experience of God. Theology is merely an attempt to explain the experience."[20] J. Gresham Machen called this mysticism: "Mysticism is the consistent exaltation of experience at the expense of thought."[21]

Personal Unhappiness

Sanford was very forthright in admitting that if she had been happy in her marriage and role as housewife and mother, she would not have become a healer: "if I had been completely satisfied with my home and family—then the work for which I was sent into the world would never have been done."[22] This is not an isolated statement. She made it clear by several frank comments that she wasn't happy in her marriage with Ted. Dissatisfaction with her role in marriage surfaced early when they didn't remain in China where all the "drudgery" of housework and child care would have been done by servants: "I explained to Ted before we were married that my consent presumed that we would remain in China. There I could continue in the work I loved—teaching—while the servants prepared meals and cleaned house and looked after babies."[23]

Sanford always regarded herself as gifted with talents in writing, painting, and drama. But she felt stifled playing the role of the wife of an Episcopalian Priest[24] and "there was always the feeling that the real me was dead."[25] After a young minister, Hollis Colwell, laid his hands on her and prayed in a positive manner for her healing, she began to have a lifting of her depression. He encouraged her to write and to let "yourself be yourself. . . . You have been trying to be a square peg in a round hole."[26] She continued counseling with Hollis, and even though "there were times after I was healed of the depression when I actually felt worse than before. . . . I was becoming a new person: the original person whom I was born to be."[27]

She started her emancipation from the straitjacket of marriage by writing two hours a day, "leaving the house and the children in Elizabeth's [her housekeeper] capable hands." Ted didn't object to this type of activity, but

> Frankly he was not pleased to see me become interested in prayer and healing. And when I began, at the request of young mothers in my Bible class to pray with the laying on of hands for their children, Ted was much disturbed . . . he looked down the years and saw me dashing here and there . . . and learning all sorts of revolutionary ideas. How right he was![28]

She found it best for four or five years not to talk to him about her "experiments in prayer."

Agnes Sanford was taught the Scriptures in the southern Presbyterian Church which subscribed to the Westminster Confession of Faith, one of the best statements of basic Christian doctrine. She alienated herself from it as a child when she was confronted by problems she felt the Church and her missionary parents seemed powerless to remedy. "Christianity had become to me words—just words—only words. And the words did not mean anything because I could see no results following them."[29] Deep depression afflicted Sanford causing her to wrestle with the questions of why we suffer and what is God's will in the midst of suffering. Added to this was her feeling that her talents were being smothered by marriage and her marital difficulties with her husband. These things—the problem of suffering and the church's inadequate response, along with her personal unhappiness—combined to form a springboard that propelled her into a "healing ministry." She desperately wanted recognition. Her determination to interpret the Bible in her own fashion led her astray, however; she looked to the wrong sources for inspiration.

Chapter Four:

New Thought, New Age, and Agnes

Among other startling statements, Agnes Sanford claimed that she was sent to this earth with a special mission ordained by God: "We come into life, I am quite sure, with sealed orders. Even at this time [childhood] the Lord was preparing me to be an explorer and a way-shower along the paths of healing and of miracles."[1] She repeated this thought five other times in *Sealed Orders.*[2]

Sanford's most astounding description of her call followed two prayers. First, John Sandford prayed for the healing of a memory that had frightened her for years: a human sacrifice she had read about in a history book as a child. Later a young woman prayed for "the opening in me of what she called the spiritual eye," and two days later the door opened "for my spirit to leap back through time."[3] She said she wasn't asleep or dreaming, "My body may have been in my study, waiting for me to come back from a meditation that became more that a meditation. But I, myself, was somewhere very far away . . . not on planet earth . . . nor was it 'heaven' as we think of heaven. I was not in a body."[4]

Then she described what can only be called an out-of-body experience (hereafter OOBE). She saw Jesus surrounded with light. He communicated with her in thought, not words. He was sending her "into a far country." There she witnessed a boy being sacrificed on an altar in Sparta, before Christ was born. Then the scene changed, and Jesus came to her again and explained that she had seen the worst happening on "planet earth" and asked her, "Would you then be willing to go down there, when I deem it best, and to be born and live on the planet for the purpose of relieving suffering? If so I must tell you it will be a hard life." This is astonishing but what follows is even more incredible.

> The sense of my heart was that I was willing. Thus I was healed in another manner. For I was never again bitter about the hardships of life nor angry with God, as I have confessed to being, remembering that this had happened long before my birth into this world: once more I could "like God." For now I knew that I myself had consented to make this earthly pilgrimage for the sake of His Son Jesus Christ.[5]

Following this account, she was quick to say she was not talking about reincarnation but immortality. However, this does not get her off the hook. She was without doubt speaking of the pre-existence of her soul which is part of the teaching of reincarnation. All New Age cults use the term *immortality* as a synonym for reincarnation so that the teaching will be acceptable to the Western mind.

Furthermore, this passage also shows she did not believe the Bible which teaches that only the Trinity—Father, Son, and Holy Spirit—existed in eternity past as I document in the next chapter. This passage also, in essence, makes her privy to the foreknowledge of God when she said she consented to make this pilgrimage for the sake of His Son Jesus Christ. In times past this was called blasphemy.

She even likened this OOBE to 2 Corinthians 12:2 where Paul speaks of being caught up into third heaven. It is also important to point out that this OOBE wasn't the first of such experiences Sanford had. As a young woman she underwent surgery, and she presumed her heart stopped "momentarily."

> The next thing I knew, I was not in my body. I was above it, just under the ceiling, looking down with a certain curiosity

at the body lying there on the operating table. Moreover, this calls to mind other memories. Did I not remember when I was a small child, the glory of a life I had known long before? Why else the waves of homesickness for "heaven" that would sweep over me? Why else the deep nostalgia . . . when singing hymns about heaven?[6]

The OOBE in which her sealed orders came followed shortly after two experiences that opened her up to the occult. The first was a "healing of the memories" prayer. She warned that "this is a very dangerous thing to do . . . with large groups. . . . As I open doors in every mind so Jesus Christ can come in, it is possible that through some open doors a destructive spirit can come in and attack me."[7] The second experience was a prayer by a young woman to open Sanford's spiritual eye—in another book Sanford calls it the "third eye."[8] The third eye is an ancient Hindu occult concept, symbolized by a mark worn in the center of the forehead. The Tibetan Djwhal, channeled through Alice Bailey, says,

> The third eye is the eye of the inner vision; director of energy or force; exists in etheric matter. One of the rules back of all magical processes is no man is a magician until the third eye is opened, for it is by means of the third eye that the thought-form is energized, directed or controlled.[9]

New Thought Healing

Sanford first met the young Episcopal minister, who later healed her, quite incidentally. He had come to their home on business to see her husband, Ted. Her baby had been sick for several weeks with an ear infection and the young Episcopal minister, Hollis Cowell, offered to say a prayer for him. He laid his hands on the child, and when the baby awoke from his nap his temperature was normal and "his ears were well." The most significant part of her description of this event is the comment she made about Hollis Colwell: "He did not argue, preach, or anyway try to convince me of the reality of spiritual healing. If he had done so, I would have stiffened in my refusal, for I was not prepared to hear this iconoclastic 'new thought.'"[10] Sanford freely admitted here that the minister who "healed" her baby and later herself was in New Thought—or the New Age movement, as it is called today.

After Hollis Colwell healed her depression, Sanford felt compelled to find the method and reason for it. She returned several times to his office when "the waves of joy receded and the darkness began to creep around the corners of my mind,"[11] and each time he prayed for her. He finally told Sanford, "In the long run, you've got to learn to pray the prayer of faith yourself." He also suggested that "one's power depended largely on eating the right foods," and therefore he and his wife "bought everything from health-food stores."[12]

Finally, she decided that "aside from diet there were other ways of receiving and passing on God's power."[13] She started on a program of "vigorous self training" in prayer and teaching "the subconscious flow of thoughts to dwell on God and not on man . . . for my subconscious had been steeped in destructive thinking."[14] She set aside all her "preconceived ideas" about the Bible and began to seek help outside the Scriptures. Apparently her first step was to read about other "adventures of faith that claimed Buddha or Mohammed or the Masters of the Far East as their inspiration."[15]

Her search for more knowledge of "spiritual healing" then led her to Christian Science:

> I did not know that there were any other books upon the subject of prayer of faith, except possibly *Science and Health*. It did not speak to my condition. Not that I scorn Christian Scientists. I am grateful to them, for at a time when the Church had totally forgotten or denied healing, they dared to believe in it.[16]

Emmet Fox Enters

Soon after her introduction to New Thought health teachings, we find this very important passage.

Then someone gave me a copy of Emmet Fox's, *The Sermon on the Mount*, and although the language of this book was not that to which I was accustomed, speaking of "treating" and "demonstrating" when I would have said "praying" and "receiving answers to prayer" still it thrilled my soul because it made clear to me the reality of the spiritual body that interpenetrates the physical body, and the spiritual world in which we really live. This book is based strongly and squarely on the words Jesus actually said.[17]

This statement compelled me to write this book. I was a disciple of the cult, Unity School of Christianity, as a young woman and cut my teeth on the writings of New Thought leader, Emmet Fox. He spoke to large audiences in London and New York City. He also lectured at Unity School of Christianity headquarters in Kansas City. When my parents travelled to New York on business, they would always plan to hear his sermons.

Anyone convinced that the Bible is the Word of God would totally reject this and all other books written by Emmet Fox. They would most emphatically say that they are not "based strongly and squarely on the words Jesus actually said." Why? Look carefully at what Fox says in *The Sermon on the Mount*:

What did Jesus teach? The plain fact is that Jesus taught no theology whatever. His teaching is entirely spiritual or metaphysical. . . . All the doctrines and theologies of the churches are human inventions. . . . Men built up a limited and man-like God who conducted his universe very much as a rather ignorant and barbarous prince might conduct the affairs of a small Oriental kingdom. Then a far-fetched and very inconsistent legend was built up concerning original sin, vicarious blood atonement, infinite punishment for finite transgressions. . . . Now, no such theory as this is taught in the Bible. The "Plan of Salvation" which figured so prominently in the evangelical sermons and divinity books of a past generation is as completely unknown to the Bible as it is to the Koran.[18]

This passage speaks for itself. From it we can say with confidence Emmet Fox did not hold to Christian doctrine. Yet in three different chapters in *Sealed Orders* and *Healing Touch of God* Sanford pays tribute to him as the most important source for her "prayer of faith" and Inner Healing. Fox himself said, "Among the various sections of the present-day Truth movement Unity is probably the most important. I am one of Mr. Fillmore's spiritual children."[19] Mr. Fillmore and his wife, Myrtle, founded Unity. Unity also denies every biblical teaching about Jesus, His divinity, His redemptive work on the cross, and His bodily resurrection.

Furthermore, when Fox explains Matthew 7:1-5, he calls it the law of retribution of Karma or the Great Law:

> It is possible to rise above even the Great Law itself, in the name of *the Christ*. In the Bible the term "Christ" is not identical with Jesus the individual. . . . It is a technical term defined as the Absolute Spiritual Truth about anything. . . . It makes no difference how deeply seated may be the trouble (sickness, poverty, weakness of character) the realization by somebody of The Christ, or the Spiritual Truth behind the appearance, will heal it. . . . So man has the choice of Karma or Christ. . . . This is the Gospel. He can remain in the limited region of matter and mind, bound fast on the wheel of Karma; or, he can appeal, through prayer, to the Realm of Spirit—that is, The Christ—and be free.[20]

This is the foundation on which Sanford built her "theology" and it bears no relationship to the Christian's foundation in Jesus Christ.

Also in this quotation, Fox repeatedly uses "The Christ" which is a buzz word in New Age writings to mean not the Messiah of Scripture but to mean, as Fox says "the Spiritual Truth behind the appearance." That Sanford knew the Unity meaning of "The Christ" may be seen from the following passage:

> One of the first things I learned was to "see the Christ" in everybody. I was perfectly able to translate that into more

ordinarily accepted terms, such as to see the highest potential for good in everyone. This is an absolute essential for healing, for by seeing the good in another person, one is able to bring it out.[21]

How similar this is to the following excerpt from a Unity booklet, "There is no better way to bless a person than to behold the Christ in him. By beholding the Christ in another person, we help him to call forth the very best in him."[22]

Larger Call

Sanford's healing ministry gradually expanded and she began to go on "occasional missions and trips" even though her husband "did not like it. . . . But the larger call drove me on, prodded me on, forced me on."[23] She obviously also enjoyed the attention: "The awareness of being loved and appreciated was most comforting to me."[24] She was now "feeling the sweep of power through me more and more, when I laid hands on someone to pray, but in praying from a distance nothing happened."[25]

Once again she searched for a key to a deeper ministry. The first step was to attend meetings at a "Chapel of Truth" in Philadelphia led by a woman who had at one time been a member of a Baptist church. From her, Sanford learned "the art of intercession." This was in 1930.

When Unity was first established, meetings were held on a week day because they didn't have "churches" yet. Sanford was only able to attend meetings held on a week day because she would be expected to attend her husband's church on Sundays.

Sanford described this teacher as a "completely Christian woman," who taught that "if people weren't healed from a distance it was because 'you are seeing them sick.'" When Sanford protested that they were sick and that's why she was praying for them, "this good lady replied, 'Yes, but unless you can learn to see them well, you only fasten the sickness upon them.'"[26] The phrase "fasten the sickness on them" brings back memories of Unity Sunday school when I learned that negative thoughts about poverty or sickness, for example, could "fasten" that very "inharmony" on me.

The Unity Guide to Healing said,

> Deny the appearance of disease or discord of any kind and realize that it is nothing. . . . Do not dwell on the details of negative conditions, for then you give them strength. Do not ask yourself, "What is wrong with me?" for then you are looking at what is wrong, not what is right. . . . It is not well to dwell upon causes of inharmony, since what we think about, even by way of persistent denials and resistance, becomes more and more part of our consciousness and hence our experience.[27]

In another place *The Unity Guide* states, "He saw the negative side of the proposition, and it weakened his demonstration. If you want to demonstrate, never consider the negative side."[28]

In the end, Fox helped her to "see that Jesus' redemption really works." She went on to say that she also found this idea treated in a practical, not theological, manner in a book called, *What Seek Ye?*, by H. B. Jefferey, another "student of truth,"[29] in other words another New Thought writer. He is identified in Myrtle Fillmore's biography as a famous speaker at Unity conventions.[30]

Chapter Five:

Agnes and God

A thought-provoking verse in the Bible, John 17:3, declares that the eternal life Jesus gives is knowledge of God: "This is life eternal, that they might know thee, the only true God, and Jesus Christ, whom thou hast sent." Christians are to know their God. This is easy to say, but how do we understand knowing God? As in our human relationships, knowing God is not merely collecting data on physical and mental characteristics, nor is it an emotional response to personality.

The basis for our concept of God is our grasp of the attributes of God as defined in Scripture. For example, the attribute of God's immutability, or unchangeability, saves us from the quagmire produced by the everchanging commandments of a situational-ethic god. Christians can rest secure in the knowledge that God does not change. His standards will hold true for eternity.

Thus, the attributes of God display much of His character. This is mirrored in human relationships as well. We come to a real knowledge of a person as we interact with them and learn about their characteristics. Then we can know if what they proclaim about themselves is really true or only empty falsehood.

God has revealed Himself to man through His Word, the Bible. Above all, we must be obedient to do what He commands. In this we glorify God. Joy and peace come to us as we obey God, and by this we "enjoy Him forever."

We also come to know God through His actions. The Old Testament especially reveals God as an acting person. God *saw* Adam's need for a companion and helpmeet, He *made* garments of skin to cover their nakedness. Noah *found favor* in the eyes of God; He *spoke* to Moses as Moses led the Israelites out of Egypt. In the New Testament, God so *loved* the world that He *gave* His only begotten Son (John 3:16). These verbs tell us about a living person who is interested as a loving father in the welfare of his children. Just as we know a friend as he reveals himself through his attributes and actions, so we come to know God as He has chosen to reveal His attributes and actions in the Bible and through the living word, Jesus Christ.

Did Agnes Sanford know God in this way? When I read her autobiography, *Sealed Orders*, and her autobiographic novel, *Lost Shepherd*, I was struck by how much her childhood years in China, where she was exposed to pagan thought, influenced her conception of God. Because of the disease, poverty, and suffering she saw there, she wrestled, as Job did, with the question of why God allows these things to happen. In an earlier chapter, I illustrated how her experience of suffering affected her ministry.

God in Nature

Sanford worshipped God as creator, but she believed that God actually dwells in and is a part of every aspect of creation, not just in regenerate men. This belief is a basic to animism, pantheism, spiritism, and the Eastern religions of Buddhism and Hinduism. It is also the foundation for the New Age belief that God is an impersonal Vital Force of Life Force, or Energy, or Light, or Divine Mind. In Hinduism, called *prana*, and in Chinese religion, called *chi*, this energy is the essence of God which permeates all matter, animate or inanimate. Sanford said, "The very chemicals contained in the body—'the dust of the earth'—live by the breath of God, by the primal energy, the original force that we call

God."[1] And, "Pure energy cannot be photographed or drawn, and God is not only pure energy but is the creator of all the light-energy from which all worlds are made."[2]

Sanford loved beauty and had a marked emotional response to the immensity of the universe and the contrasted delicacy of a flower. She called herself a practical mystic. So certain statements she made in her books can be taken in this light:

> Twice during these two summers of my early teens, God spoke to me, though I did not know at the time it was He, for He did not speak in any way that one would expect . . . not on Sunday morning nor on Sunday afternoon [when] we settled in a circle in the living room to study the Bible. One time I had climbed to the highest valley . . . rough grass filled the valley, and I lay upon it in the full sun and what I thought about I do not know. But in some way . . . I entered into a state of indescribable dreamy bliss wherein I was part of the tall crisp grass, and with the tiny creatures that lived within it, and with the high blue sky whence sunlight drenched my body with pure joy. There was no more time. It was yesterday and today and forever. There was no more me as a separate being. I was part of the tall grass and the tiny sounds when it crinkled in the sun sounded within myself also, as truly did the beating of my heart.[3]

This may possibly be just an emotional response to God's creation but the second episode she described that took place the next summer is a clear statement of pagan belief:

> One other time I felt this indescribable presence of God the Creator. Again I was alone, but this time active, exploring a rocky slope. . . . While scrambling over the rocks, I entered into a state of high ecstacy that was not entirely of this world. . . . It was rather the uncreated essence of the Creator, His ever-living creativity, flowing into me from bamboo and from rock from fern and moss and tiny orchids hiding in the grass. I did not know it at the time, for I had no idea that sentient life of any kind could be in things inanimate. But it

can be—it is. The life of the Creator is in every created thing, for it is made of the very essence of His being, and His word from whence it came still speaks through grass and grasshoppers to those attuned to Him.[4]

This is not just an isolated quotation. Sanford expresses this same theology in all her books.

They [Christian Scientists] say, God is the creative principle, and we have and can use the creative principle. There is a shred of truth in this, of course. But this is only a small part of the whole great truth. God is not only in us or the sun or the rocks or the trees. God is.[5]

So I explained to Sammy that there was a healing energy in him that the doctors called nature and that this same healing life was in the world outside of him, too. . . . Ask God. Because He is the one who made nature, and He's in nature, and He is nature.[6]

She, who knew God as a palpitating force, filling every blade of grass and every golden aspen. [7]

Within a rock there is the high shining light of God. But the rock does not know that the light of God is within it.[8]

Certainly, we may see God as Creator when we observe nature but that is vastly different than saying God is nature. Sanford never changed her mind about this, for she wrote in her last book when she was in her eighties: "Not only is the light of God so present in my plants that people wonder what kind of fertilizer I use, but also this same light flows between me and all living things."[9]

Pre-existence of the Soul

Sanford also believed in the pre-existence of the soul, another belief which runs counter to the clear teachings of

Scripture. The pre-existence of the soul is a key element of the doctrine of reincarnation and such cults as Mormonism. The Bible says that only the Godhead existed in eternity past (Gen. 1:1; Ps. 90:2, 93:2; John 1:1). Sanford asks,

> Why does beauty comfort and still my soul? Is it because this reflects the beauty and order of that heavenly kingdom from which the soul has come, and therefore fills the unconscious being with the unreasonable reassurance of a life that is from everlasting?[10]

She was saying that the soul comes from heaven and has existed in eternity past. She denied that she believed in reincarnation yet made a statement which shows otherwise.

> Even for us it may be harder to be born than to die. Since the spirit is breathed into us by God, who knows how and in what manner that spirit may have lived before drawing near to this earth? Since there is no time with God and since we are heirs of immortality, who shall say when our spirits evolved from the Godhead, speeded forth at His word. Who shall say where they may have lived and in what manner they may have served Him before they were sent upon this desperate journey of life on earth?[11]

If, as she said, our spirits evolved from the Godhead we would be divine.

> There is no explaining the effect the ocean has always had upon my heart or unconscious self, Does my spirit remember? Was I really there in God when the seas separated themselves from the land and went into their own place?[12]

We did not pre-exist. We were created in our mother's womb (Ps. 139:12-16). Our spirit does not pre-exist for God breathed into Adam the breath of life at the time He formed him from the dust of the earth.

Sanford denied so many times in her books and tapes that she believed in reincarnation it is obvious she was tarred frequently with that brush. She claimed that she would never want to return to this planet and therefore she was not a believer in reincarnation. However, coupling her belief in the pre-existence of her soul with her belief she would be sent to another planet after her death, makes her denials rather empty. She speculated that the spirit may not stay in heaven after death but may be sent by God to serve him on other planets:

> Then I awoke, and even now I am filled with joy when I think of this dream, and I know that whatever it may have meant to my subconscious mind, the real meaning of it was to tell my spirit something about the many mansions of heaven. Can it be that after a time of rest by the 'still waters' and of rejoicing before the throne of grace, we may be asked to go to some new planet that has never even heard of Jesus and to take them His love?[13]

She also quoted in several of her books from Wordsworth's "Intimations of Immortality," a poem which speaks of reincarnation.

Universal Fatherhood of God

When studying Sanford's books, her confusion about the attributes of God becomes apparent in her statements about the fatherhood of God. She quoted Scripture and made biblical statements such as, "For here is truth: sin separates us from God and dims the power of our prayers."[14] But we must balance a rare outburst of orthodoxy with the many assertions that everyone is a child of God.

She viewed the fatherhood of God as being a universal fatherhood. "Some nations have willed to dominate others, and some nations have willed to live alone and make money regardless of others. Both of these wills are incompatible with the will of God, who says that we are one in Him."[15] There is no mistaking she was speaking from her belief in God as universal Father.

Further on in the same chapter she exhorted her readers

to pray for the leaders of the nations and "send the love of Christ into their minds. Through this love of Christ we call forth the potential goodness that is in them because it is in all men."[16] Scripture does not contain one verse that says we can send the love of Christ into the mind of a natural man. In fact the Scriptures indicate otherwise: "The natural man receiveth not the things of the Spirit of God; neither can he know them because they are spiritually discerned" (1 Cor. 2:14). Similarly, "Because the carnal mind is enmity against God: for it is not subject to the law of God, neither indeed can be" (Rom. 8:7). Only the Holy Spirit has the power to enter the mind of an unbeliever to draw him to Himself.

Sanford was clever at camouflaging her foundational beliefs about God by intermixing them with Christian terms. However, the passages quoted in this chapter make a solid case for saying she was a pantheist who believed in the universal fatherhood of God and pre-existence of the soul. Her writings show she believed in some form of reincarnation, though she also denied it and wrote much about heaven. These two things are not compatible if we understand the biblical doctrine of the future life.

Chapter Six:

A Blurred Picture of Jesus

The picture Sanford painted of Jesus, the second person of the Godhead, is as blurred as her portrayal of the Godhead as a whole. In an effort, I suppose, to make her writing colorful, she used some unusual, almost disrespectful synonyms for Jesus: Transformer (electrical), Heavenly plumber, psychologist, our time traveler, the one who knew, Light Bearer.

Beyond this, she distorted the biblical portrait of Jesus as Saviour and the part that His shed blood plays in our salvation. As a child she reacted against her parents' beliefs, and one time she left the dinner table in tears because her parents were critical of Harry Emerson Fosdick, the noted theological liberal of that time, when he came to China and preached on Christian love in their church. According to Sanford, her parents disliked him "because he did not mention the blood of the Lamb in every third sentence."[1]

In her twenties, while teaching in an Episcopal school for girls, Sanford found "they never referred to the Blood of the Lamb" and she "found this a certain relief."[2] She did wonder if they were orthodox. Years later, when a young man at her School of Pastoral Care complained that the "trouble with this school is I have to re-think my whole theology," Sanford replied that the teaching of healing "includes a re-examination of one's beliefs concerning God and a deepened understanding of the mind of man."[3]

The Lamb's Energized Blood

She wrote that some look with tolerance on books which proclaim that Christ's robe and the silver chalice and other holy relics still radiate His life. She follows with, "then why should not His blood be filled with a life-energy? Matter is indestructible, also that matter is energy. "

> [T]his moving energy was first encompassed in the visible flow of blood and water. Very soon the water evaporated and became an invisible vapor vibrant with His life. Very soon the clotted blood dried into dust, and was disseminated by the wind and mingled with all life so that it could no longer be seen. But the life in the blood is indestructible and still remains an invisible current of a heavenly energy, an actual energy, a perceptible energy and effective energy. That heavenly energy still remains in the air that we breathe.[4]

If, as she claimed, His blood is heavenly energy and is in the air we breathe, then we are once again back to Eastern religion in disguise. Yoga places great emphasis on correct breathing because some Hindus believe we breathe the universal (god) force called prana which is in the air around us. Proper breathing helps to balance the life forces within us, giving us peace and health. Sanford goes on to say in this passage on the blood:

> This heavenly energy which is different from the universal love of the Father, supplies our needs for the healing of memories—the freeing of the subconscious mind—the integrating of the personality—the bringing forth of the creative energies—all those things we madly seek . . . from psychiatrists, hospitals and rest homes. . . . In the words of the Bible, the forgiveness of sins.[5]

Redemption in Gethsemane

Stranger yet is Sanford's theology of redemption. She explained the event of Gethsemane as the beginning of the redemptive work of Jesus on the cross.

He had to reach the subconscious mind, or the heart, of every human being. For the barrier between God and man was in the heart. . . . The channel from spirit to subconscious was like a canal choked by gathered sand and silt. . . . Jesus opened that channel. . . . But in order to redeem the human race it was necessary to sink deeper into humanity; to become part of the subconscious mind of every man. . . . Hitherto He had turned His heart always toward God. . . . In the Garden of Gethsemane He reversed this process. . . . He turned away from God's light and let His spirit sink into man's darkness. . . . All the griefs and sorrows of mankind rolled in on Him, and He permitted that they should do so. No wonder that the sweat . . . was as great drops of blood. Surely the death that ended on Calvary began in Him now. . . . Not only in the Garden did He bear our sins and carry our sorrows . . . and in the Garden of Gethsemane where He delivered that fatal wound [to the serpent's head] by becoming part of evil that He might destroy evil.[6]

There are several obvious errors in these statements when compared to the Bible, and she gave no Scripture verses to buttress her text. Sanford totally ignored the biblical fact of God's anger toward sin and that propitiation means averting God's wrath by an offering. This is graphically portrayed in the Old Testament rituals of the sin offering, trespass (guilt) offering and day of atonement (Lev. 12:12,13,24,25; 23:27,28). Romans 1:18 says, "For the wrath of God is revealed from heaven against all ungodliness and unrighteousness of men, who hold the truth in unrighteousness." But "God commended his love toward us, in that, while we were yet sinners, Christ died for us. Much more then, being now justified by his blood, we shall be saved from the wrath to come" (Rom. 5:8-9). The New Testament portrays Jesus as the innocent Lamb taking the place of guilty sinners—a substitution—that we might be accepted as righteous in Him (John 1:29, 1 Pet. 1:19, Rev. 5).

Furthermore, she made the statement that "Death might have come to Him from strain and suffering even if He had remained in the garden. . . . Why did He not stay in the garden among His disciples instead of being made a public spectacle?"[7] It was prophesied Jesus would die as a sacrifice, but Sanford ignored the Bible. She said Jesus didn't stay in the garden to finish our redemption because if He had stayed no one would have believed He had really died and been resurrected. Apparently for her the only reason for the cross was the public spectacle it would make.

In Gethsemane, Jesus did not turn away from God as Sanford says, but accepted his will. Later we shall see that Sanford's idea of Jesus entering into the subconscious of men in Gethsemane is essential to her theory of Healing of Memories.

At one time she believed she would never die physically because of her "sealed orders"[8] to bring a "new gospel . . . the gospel of healing."[9] Her reasoning for this possibility involved conjecture about the nature of the resurrection body. She started her reasoning with what happens to the blood of Christ as we have already quoted her. Then she turned to how Jesus resurrected His body.

> He must have gathered all His spiritual powers and focused them upon His lifeless body seeing it from without, as some of us have done when near death, that it might be transformed into the new order of being. He had left the greater part of His blood on earth, to be for man an ever-increasing current of power . . . for the forgiveness of sins. Therefore, the body of Christ in the tomb not only had to be resurrected cell by cell, but also presumably the process of making blood had to be tremendously speeded up, so that as nature replenishes the blood of one who has given a blood transfusion, so nature should replenish His blood stream—after the blood transfusion that He gave to humanity.[10]

Her tortuous reasoning became even more esoteric:

> Two physical processes take place at the same time in a man who believes in Jesus Christ: the process of losing energy in the body and the process of renewing strength in the spirit.

> If life works fast enough in the spirit it can overtake and
> transcend the death process in the body . . . that the new
> order of being of which Christ was the first fruits, can be
> achieved without the pain of death.[11]

She was saying, in essence, if we achieve holiness quickly enough
through our own efforts, we will receive our glorified body
here on earth.

Sanford, in reality, preached good works as a requirement for becoming right with God. She never seemed to
understand what happened when Jesus died on the cross as
our substitute and paid the penalty with His shed blood for
our sin; that those who trust in Christ's righteousness are judged
righteous because Jesus satisfied all of God's righteous de-
mands upon the sinner (Rom. 3:22-26, 5:1). Christians do sin
while on earth, but Jesus is our Advocate before God. If we
confess our sins, God will forgive them (1 John 1:9). If Christians, however, do not repent but wilfully continue to sin,
there is a loss of fellowship with the Father and Son and
grieving of the Holy Spirit. There will be loss of blessing,
chastisement, or even physical death (Heb. 12:6, 1 Cor. 11:30).

She seemed to believe in redemption when she stated,
"He makes us righteous," quoting Romans 4:22-24. She also
said,

> According to Revelation 22:15, He does not impute righ-
> teousness to those who persist in lying, stealing, murder-
> ing, and sexual immorality. Time would fail me to enumer-
> ate the Bible passages that tell us that the wages of sin is
> death but the gift of God is eternal life through Jesus Christ
> our Lord. (Romans 6:23) Does that mean . . . "Go on
> sinning, little children, it is all right for I will see that you go
> to heaven just the same"? On the contrary, He has given us
> a most strict and rigorous way of life that we must live in
> order to attain eternity.[12]

While we have been given a "most strict and rigorous
way of life" to follow, this is not the ground of our salvation.

Rather, the ground of our salvation is in the efforts of Christ, not our own. We can do nothing by ourselves to attain eternity.

She quoted Romans 6:23 but obviously didn't really believe it. Apparently she didn't know eternal life begins the moment we are justified and regenerated (John 3:1-7, 15). As natural birth cannot be reversed, so spiritual birth cannot be reversed. Out of her disbelief in the eternal security of the saints came her doctrine of the sons of God.

Sons of God

The Bible uses the phrase "sons of God" twelve times. Sanford chose to base her ideas about this phrase primarily on just one verse: "For the earnest expectation of the creature waiteth for the manifestation of the sons of God" (Rom. 8:19). She cited this verse repeatedly throughout her books. She often used it in relationship to a kingdom of heaven on earth brought about through the agency of the sons of God who will never die and will live on earth eternally.

Sanford's insecurity about her final destination is evident in her thinking about the sons of God. She wrote a chapter on Job in her book, *Healing Power of the Bible*. When Satan comes before God to consider Job, the sons of God are present (Job 1:1, 2:1). Sanford rightly called the sons of God "great and mysterious beings." She followed this with a debatable statement: "Some of them, through the power and operation of the Holy Spirit, will emerge in and through living people upon the earth and for this the whole creation abides, waiting for the manifestation of the sons of God (Romans 8:19)."[13]

She carried this theme into a chapter on Adam and Eve, "The Creator's crowning experiment upon this planet seems to be to bring forth a being both physical and also spiritual, in hopes that among this race there may evolve the sons of God (John 1:12)."[14] This suggests, of course, God did not have a plan when He created Adam and further that the sons of God would evolve.

Speaking once more of Adam, Sanford stated, "Apparently God had in mind a plan for man's evolving step by step into a being not subject to death."[15] Obviously Sanford's claim is wrong because God told Adam he would die *only if* he disobeyed God and ate of the tree of the knowledge of good and evil (Gen. 2:17).

Later, in a chapter about Ananias and Sapphira, she was concerned with the sin rampant in our modern world. She pointed out there are "some people great in prayer and power . . . master-builders: who so care for their Lord that they are willing to undertake and carry on the rigorous training for the life of the Spirit that will enable them to become the sons of God . . . making peace upon this earth."[16] It is evident she was speaking about Christians because they "care for the Lord." Yet they will only obtain the special status of sons of God through works or evolving spiritually as Sanford puts it. These sorts of distortions regarding redemption are clearly outside the realm of Christian thinking.

Chapter Seven:

Flirting with Spiritism

During her searches in New Thought, Sanford also dabbled in Spiritism. She went with an "eminent Quaker" to a "prayer group wherein one communicated directly with the departed at the home of a real Christian family and every meeting began with prayer and was carried on in the name of Christ."[1] After the seance ended she "went home strangely unaffected either for good or for ill."[2] At the next visit she prayed for the medium's mother and felt assured she would be healed of her heart ailment. The medium rode home with her on the same subway and they discussed the seance. Sanford noted the "odor on his breath was intolerable." The next day she felt terrible, "drained of life," and she could taste in her own mouth that same terrible odor. Frightened she resolved to never "go near a seance again . . . much to the irritation of some of my friends, who consider me narrowminded."[3]

She continued, however, to "join in prayer with those involved in spiritualism" and even went to Washington D.C. with three friends to a prayer meeting which turned out to be a seance. She participated knowing that one of the women was a medium. As time went on she found that four people she prayed with, who were involved with spiritism, died or were seriously hurt in accidents: "Whatever the explanation, I was evidently not a good person to pray with, or for, anyone involved in spiritualism."[4]

From that time on she and Ted did not allow persons

who had participated in spiritualism to enroll at the School of Pastoral Care. She does not say she should have refused to go to the first or subsequent seances because the Bible specifically forbids it (Lev. 19:31, 20:6, 27; Deut. 18:11-12), rather, this decision was made only because of fear for what might happen to her friends.

It is very evident Sanford had a wide friendship with persons in the occult. She was either ignorant of God's injunction against involvement with mediums or deliberately disobeyed Him. Whatever the reason, we have several other examples of times when Sanford opened her mind to spiritistic influence.

In one of her books, Sanford admitted further association with spiritism when she attended Christian conferences where "books about Edgar Cayce, and other spiritualistic literature were for sale along with my books."[5] She said she was horrified at this.

Sanford was well aware of the controversial nature of her ministry: "The churches still looked askance at me since I proclaimed the heretical news that Jesus lives and heals today."[6] Actually, no Christian denies the fact that Jesus is alive and God heals. However, the issue is whether Sanford was God's chosen vessel to proclaim a new Gospel, that of healing.

In her several books, she mentioned many people who influenced her ministry and life, but there is a marked absence of evangelical Christians, except for her parents, on this list. Some are not considered part of orthodox Christianity at all, such as John Gaynor Banks, Brother Rufus Moseley, Dr. Worchester of the Immanuel Movement, Dr. Robert Bell, and Glen Clark.

In particular, Glen Clark encouraged Sanford by publishing her first book, *The Healing Light*, when no other publisher would. He also invited her to be a speaker and leader of some of his Camps Farthest Out meetings. In Clark's own book, *God's Reach*, he writes of the Seven Dimensions of Man and how they resemble the steps to perfection of Theosophy. His terminology is pure New Thought. He portrays Jesus as a superlative teacher of parables and an example of a perfected man.

A quote from *God's Reach* makes clear his theology of works,

> In Part I we examined the stairways by which man, born as a son of earth, may climb into sonship with God. . . . God sent His Son into this world to show us the way the human and divine may be blended in perfectly adjusted and harmonious relationship with his God and in perfect rhythm with his fellow man.[7]

In the entire book there is no mention of sin, only disharmony, and there is silence about becoming sons of God through receiving Jesus who shed His blood to reconcile us to God.

In one of his more mysterious statements he seems to say that all religions are equal:

> The psalms in the orthodox churches, the affirmations of the New Thought centers, the mantrams of the eastern religions all have the purpose of impressing, through repetition, upon the subconscious mind, the great cosmic truths of life.[8]

Jungian Connection

Sanford introduced her personal pastor in her later years, Morton T. Kelsey, to Inner Healing. Kelsey and her minister son, John Sanford (not to be confused with John Sandford), also studied at the Jung Institute in Zurich and thus were influenced by Carl G. Jung, the psychiatrist. Jung was involved in the occult and was a believer in reincarnation. Fathered by a protestant minister, he wrote in *Modern Man in Search of a Soul*, "the spiritual catastrophe of the Reformation put an end to the Gothic Age."[9]

Very aware of Jung's teachings, Sanford used Jung's terminology and examples in her books, especially in *The Healing Power of the Bible* and *The Healing Gifts of the Spirit*. The most common of Jung's concepts which she used is that of the collective consciousness of mankind, or as Sanford expressed it, "mass subconscious of the race,"[10] "mass-mind of humanity,"[11] and "the old inherited mind within us."[12]

Sanford gave a "Christian" overlay to blatant Jungian concepts in the following passage from *The Healing Gifts of the Spirit*,

> For now we know that we have within us another mind than the conscious, and this unconscious mind is not disconnected from life but is connected with the mind of the race: the collective unconscious. Therefore we can 'pick up' thoughts and impressions from another or from life outside ourselves or from the memories of the race. Now into this collective unconscious, into these race memories, Jesus Christ entered, and there he lived during the days we rightly call Passion Week.... Our Lord, when He took our sins and sorrows into Himself, made the connection with all of us. He became forever a part of the mass mind of the race, so that even though His living being is now in heaven at the right hand of the Father, a part of His consciousness is forever bound up with the deep mind of man.[13]

Besides showing her knowledge of Jungian thought, this quotation has several errors in Christian theology. First, she said Jesus took our sins *into* Himself not *upon* Himself. This means Jesus became sinful, and thus, He would be powerless over sin and no longer a spotless Lamb fit to pay the penalty for our sin. Then she says he became forever a part of the mass mind of God which suggests that Jesus was only man, not God-man. God cannot become part of the mass mind which is a cesspool of sin.

Also note in the above passage when she speaks of picking up thoughts from another person, or extra-sensory perception. To use the newest New Age term, this is *psi phenomena*.

Sanford uses the word *numinous* many times. Although Jung borrowed the term from Rudolph Otto's *The Idea of the Holy*, it is usually associated with Jung. He defined it as what human beings experience when in contact with God. It is also another term for God—the numinous. Sanford equated numinous with the Holy Spirit, "I do not think he mentioned such numinous matters as the Holy Spirit."[14] Several times Sanford showed her familiarity with Jung by utilizing numinous to describe some of her mystical experiences. Her familiarity with Jung went beyond use of similar language.

> I think C.G. Jung explains the matter thus: a person can unconsciously build in himself a little house of hate . . . a personal problem of hate, which can be caused from his own indulgence in feeling and expressing hate. Then it is possible for an entity from without, a thought-form of hate, to come in and live in that house.[15]

Occultic Terminology

In this quotation, Sanford dug a deeper hole for herself than just quoting Jung. She used the word "thought-form" several times in her writings. Thought-form is a word coined by Theosophy. Annie Besant, who became the leader of Theosophy after Madame Blavatsky's death, published a book in 1901 entitled *Thought Forms*, in collaboration with a homosexual clergyman, C. W. Leadbeater, who was an early disciple of Theosophy.

Madame Blavatsky, who founded Theosophy, was born in Russia into a family of minor nobility. At an early age she first demonstrated psychic powers and later was exorcised by several priests. She married General Blavatsky who was over twenty years older than she. The marriage was a disaster from the start. Still in her teens, she fled Russia and spent the next twenty years in the Middle East and India learning the black arts and perfecting her ability as a medium. In 1873, she arrived in New York City and two years later founded the

Theosophical Society with the help of several prominent people who were interested in spiritism.

Theosophy teaches embraces reincarnation and Karmaand teaches that Jesus is an Ascended Master. Along with Transcendentalism, Theosophy has been a dominant influence on the New Age Movement and such New Thought cults as Unity School of Christianity, Unitarianism, Christian Science, Science of Mind, and Silva Mind Control. Jung commented, "The modern movement which is numerically most impressive is undoubtedly Theosophy, together with its continental sister Anthroposophy; these are pure Gnosticism in a Hindu dress."[16]

The concept of thought-forms is that each definite thought produces a double effect—a radiating vibration and a floating form. When the radiating vibrations strike another mental body they tend to provoke in it their own rate of motion and thus produce in that mind similar thoughts. This is also sometimes known as clairvoyance. The second effect of thought is the creation of a definite form. Besant and Leadbeater have thirty-eight color drawings in their book of various thoughts seen by psychics, and they bemoan the fact that the drawings can't depict the thought forms in three dimensions as they really appear.

W. Brugh Joy M.D., a Mayo-trained specialist in internal medicine, says in his New Age best-selling book, *Joy's Way*,

> the human psyche is capable of creating thought forms (forms in thought) that can influence matter, including the human body. Now I want to talk about the similar process of creating entities—fields of energy that can appear to take on the form of a human, or animal or an angelic being, a demon or even an Inner Teacher.[17]

He explains further:

> Every time an individual images a person in his or her mind, a subtle form of the imagined person is created . . . but people who are highly developed in the art of thought-form

creation can empower their thought-forms with enough energy to materialize them.[18]

As evidenced by the illustration given above, Jung agreed with this idea about thought-forms when he says "an entity without, a thought-form" can come into a person. In New Age or occult terminology an entity is a spirit or demonic being. In commenting about her father's experiences in China with demonic spirits, Sanford said, "although he did not see them, he had come to know the terrible reality of these thought-forms and had learned from a country minister how to exorcise them."[19] Sanford knew what thought forms meant, yet she used this terminology several times in relation to her theology of prayer as we will illustrate in the section on her prayer of faith.

Another word invented by Theosophy and picked up by Unity and other New Thought cults is *at-one-ment* which makes a mongrel of the meaning of the atonement of Jesus. They use it in the sense of realizing we are God, complete harmony, becoming God.

Sanford used *at-one-ment* and unfortunately it is also in the vocabulary of some Christian ministers. Alice Bailey, leader of Theosophy following Anne Besant, uses this term in her numerous books written as she channeled her spirit guide, Djwhal Khul. Carl Jung, Emmet Fox, Unity writers, and Ernest Holmes, founder of Science of Mind, all used *at-one-ment* but not in the biblical sense of the work of Christ. Christ's work dealt with the problem posed by man's sin separating him from a holy God, and bringing sinners into a right relationship with God. An example of the manner in which *at-one-ment* was used can be taken from Charles Fillmore: "Some degree of at-one-ment between mind and its organ, the brain, is required to bring about the fulfillment of our ideals."[20]

Aura is another favorite word of Sanford, and she employs it in the occult sense of seeing energy or light surrounding a person or object. Sanford recounted an incident when she was in Australia to illustrate the "many ways God has of making His presence known." A minister took a picture without a flash in the darkness of a little chapel in the bush country but the "photograph showed a ball of gentle light gleaming in the center of the alter." She showed the snapshot to a lady later in Sydney and "she said simply, 'Quite. I saw that light in the cathedral while you were lecturing.'"[21] In another book she said, "I too have seen it [a halo] around the head of a lecturer or preacher caught up in the joy of the Lord. It looks exactly like the halos depicted in some of the ancient paintings of Jesus or His mother."[22]

Notice how closely this resembles what Theosophist, C. W. Leadbeater says in *Man Visible and Invisible*, his book about clairvoyance,

> Yellow light signifies the intellect. When this color is present in the oval (aura), it invariably shows itself in the upper part, in the neighborhood of the head; consequently it is the origin of the idea of the nimbus round the head of a saint—for when any person of some development is making a special effort of any kind, as in preaching or lecturing, the intellectual faculties are in unusual activity, and the yellow glow is intensified. No doubt it was either from occasional glimpses of this phenomenon or from traditions derived from those who could see (clairvoyantly), that our medieval painters derived the idea of the glory round the head of a saint.[23]

This same thought is conveyed by another quote from Sanford, "The mind also projects. The whole church was filled with an emanation, a radiation, of a spiritual power."[24]

Twice she talked about her times of "meditation looking through the gardens and to the top of the little hill and as I meditated on the light of God, I could often see a light like an aura around the birch trees."[25] These are but a few references to an aura-like emanation found in her writings. Taken alone, her use of the word *aura* as an occultist uses it, would not be significant. It is damaging, however, when one adds this to the pervasive influence of the New Age on her religious teaching.

Chapter Eight:

Prayer of Faith

Agnes Sanford believed she was divinely commissioned to preach the "Gospel of Healing" through her "sealed orders." Neither Jesus nor the entire canon of Scripture as inspired by God mention of a "Gospel of Healing." None of the prophetic books predict that a "Gospel of Healing" would be preached in the future. In the New Testament, the Gospel was proclaimed to Joseph before the birth of Christ when the angel told Joseph to name the child Jesus for "he shall save his people from their sins" (Matt. 1:21). This is the "good news" or Gospel: that Jesus Christ came in the flesh, lived a sinless life, and died on the cross as a sacrifice for our sins that we might be reconciled to a holy God.

The other gospels mentioned in the Bible tie in with this basic Gospel: gospel of the Kingdom (Matt 4:23, 24:14); gospel of God (Rom. 1:1, 15:16; 1 Thess. 2:8; 1 Tim. 1:11; 1 Pet. 4:17); gospel of Jesus Christ (seven references from Mark 1:1 to Phil. 1:27); gospel of Grace (Acts 20:24); gospel of Salvation (Eph. 1:13); and gospel of Peace with God (Eph. 6:15).

Furthermore Jesus said He came to do the

will of him that sent me. And this is the Father's will which hath sent me, that of all which he hath given me I should lose nothing but should raise it up again at the last day. And this is the will of him who sent me, that every one which seeth the Son, and believeth on him, may have everlasting life: and I will raise him up at the last day (John 6:38-40).

The central pivot around which Sanford built her "gospel" was the prayer of faith. Sanford based her conviction that her prayer of faith was valid not on biblical doctrine, although she does quote a few New Testament verses, but she based it on experience. In her own words, "Experience comes before theology,"[1] and "[r]eligion is a matter of experiencing God."[2] Therefore, her prayer of faith grew out of her own emotional experience of "healing":

> The minister laid his hands on my head and prayed for the healing of my mental depression quite as simply and naturally as he had prayed for the healing of Jack's ears. And it happened immediately! All heaven broke loose upon me and within me![3]

Only after Sanford had this overwhelming experience did she search the Scriptures to try to legitimize her experience from the words of Jesus. She made her conclusion first and then looked for the evidence. This is contrary to any valid secular or scientific research or for sound biblical exegesis. She also emphasized common sense, "use your own searchlight of common sense and inspired wondering, and that as you do so passages hitherto puzzling will be highlighted by truth."[4] Common sense can mislead us. Apparently, Jesus' words didn't really satisfy her quest for evidence about healing through "the prayer of faith" since she then turned to the Masters of the East, Christian Science, and Unity as I have shown previously.

Sanford referred to her prayer of healing over and over again as "the prayer of faith," not a prayer of faith or praying in faith. Sanford justified her prayer of faith based on James 5:15: "And the prayer of faith shall save the sick, and the Lord shall raise him up; and if he have committed sins, they shall be forgiven him." But verse 14 says the sick should call for the *elders* and they are to pray over him and anoint him with oil in the name of the Lord. Her prayer does not, by any stretch of the imagination, resemble James 5:14-15.

Instead did she designate her prayer in this manner because of her ties with Unity? Or was it a coincidence? The biography of Myrtle Fillmore, titled *Mother of Unity*, has a section on "The Prayer of Faith":

> The August 1898 issue of "Wee Wisdom" was a milestone in another respect, too. In that edition the most popular single item in the history of Unity publishing appeared for the first time. It was untitled, and Mrs. Fillmore didn't know its author, but it was later determined to be "The Prayer of Faith" written by Hannah More Kohous.

Mrs. Fillmore met Mrs. Kohous in 1905 who explained,

> she had first written the piece for a Chicago Truth magazine ... and it had been the very first output from her pen after she was born into the Truth of being. ... It was Mrs. Kohous who clothed these mighty statements of Truth in such simple rhythmic garb that the tiniest tot can say them. Thus "The Prayer of Faith" was assured of its place in what Mrs. Fillmore called a "part of the metaphysical scriptures". ... Even today, the first thing taught in many Unity primary Sunday School classes is "The Prayer of Faith."[5]

Sanford probably learned of this prayer at the Chapel of Truth in Philadelphia which she attended weekly beginning in 1930.

In the beginning of Sanford's ministry, her prayer of faith was fairly simple, patterned after Hollis Colwell's prayer. Later in her ministry, though, it became "a more intense and advanced meditation toward contacting God's life."[6] At first she laid her hands on the persons seeking help, usually standing behind them. Then she would pray in an affirmative manner commanding God's power to come into their body and heal them. Next, she thanked God, stated she knew God would do what she asked, and "saw" the diseased body part well as

"You made it to be." Finally, she ended her prayers with, "So be it" or "So it is," as a term of commanding God to do that for which she had just prayed. Early on, she was adamant that to be successful in prayer one should not say, "If it be thy will" for that showed lack of faith. In later years, however, she did decide it was acceptable to say, "according to thy will." She admitted in her autobiography that in the beginning she "was not prepared to hear this iconoclastic 'new thought' (It was old as the hills really, but I did not know it)."[7]

"Many points were perplexing to me as I tried to pursue the path of faith."[8] Possibly, this was due to her unusual thoughts about faith. For example, one time when she spilled boiling water on her foot she claimed the power of the Spirit and

> stated by faith that the skin of my foot was not burned and it was not! At this time some people may be thinking, "But isn't this metaphysics? Isn't this the power of positive thinking?" Certainly! And I might point out that Jesus called it faith.[9]

The first requirement of biblical faith is that it must be directed toward God and that the person must have confidence that God fulfills the promises He makes to us as revealed in the Bible. Next, faith in God requires knowledge of His attributes so we have a basis for trusting Him. This is why Romans 10:17 says, "So then faith cometh from hearing and hearing by the word of God." In order to possess faith one must be born into the family of God because, "But the natural man receiveth not the things of the Spirit of God, for they are foolishness unto him; neither can he know them for they are spiritually discerned" (1 Cor. 2:14).

In another place Sanford said, "the sufferer may say, 'But I don't have any faith.' 'That's all right,' I respond. 'I can have faith for you'. . . . We can interpose our own faith for the faithlessness of another!"[10] Carried to its logical conclusion this would mean every nonbeliever could be saved through

the faith of a believer, making salvation through the blood
of Jesus unnecessary. Having faith for someone else is rather
similar to the Mormon belief of salvation through baptism
for the dead.

In the same vein, when a person was unable to remember past bitterness she wrote,

> So I thought, "I will repent of them in her name. I will say
> to Jesus, 'Let the grown woman go free, for I will take the
> responsibility for her sins of fear and hate. Since she cannot
> see them to repent of them herself, I will repent of them in
> her name, and so open the door for the forgiveness of
> God.'"[11]

Sanford now had her prayer of faith but still "many points
were perplexing as I tried to pursue the path of faith."[12] The
two most perplexing questions were how to contact the power
and what was the mechanism that made the prayer of faith
work. This is why she was so excited to find the answers
given by Unity lecturer Emmet Fox. She found the answer—
the revelation of "the reality of the spiritual body"—in his
book, *The Sermon on the Mount*:

> It thrilled my soul because it made clear to me the reality of
> the spiritual body that interpenetrates the physical body, and
> of the spiritual world in which we really live.... This idea of
> the spiritual body and the physical body, and of the Spirit
> of God permeating the spiritual body is the very foundation stone of the whole Bible.[13]

This type of statement was not isolated to only one quote or
even only one book:

> Then the tremendous truth dawned on me (and it is nothing
> new, but has been since the beginning) that this spiritual
> body is part of me now, co-existing with the physical body.[14]

Scripture does teach that humans have a created, but not
divine, spiritual aspect to our material body, but it reserves

the language of "spiritual body" for the resurrection of the dead (1 Cor. 15) or to those who are alive at Christ's return (1 Thes. 4:15-17). In the above passage, she also said man has had a spiritual body from the beginning, that is, at creation in Genesis 2:7, for "into man, there was breathed the sentient and creative Spirit of God—we are not one person but two—the spiritual body interpenetrates the body of flesh."[15] Chapters later she repeated this theme, "In the beginning we are made double beings: of the dust of the earth, and of the breath of God. We are two bodies living together, the spiritual body interpenetrating the flesh."[16] Again, her thinking was contrary to Scripture for Genesis doesn't teach that God poured an aspect of His own being into mankind. Creator and creature are distinct kinds of beings. Had creation taken place as Sanford indicated, Adam would have been a part of God not a human made in the image of God as the Scripture says (Gen. 1:27).

At first I didn't understand the full implication of these statements as they affected her prayer of faith until I read her concept of the Body of Christ in yet another one of her books.

> The spirits of all who enter into the new life become one body, the body of Christ on earth. It is achieved by an actual merging of our spirits into His Spirit, so that He abides in us and we in Him (John 15:4). This cannot mean that our bodies enter into His physical body, and it certainly does not mean merely that we join a body of people called a church. It means what it says as clearly as words can say them: that our real selves, our spirits, become actually a part of His spiritual body.[17]

This was also a subtle promotion of her pantheistic belief that we are God because, as she said, there is a merging of our spirits into His Spirit. *To merge* means to be absorbed into something else, to be combined or consolidated. In contrast, the Bible teaches when we accept Jesus as our Saviour and Lord the Holy Spirit comes to dwell in us but not to be

an actual part of us—just as we dwell in a home but we are
not actually the home itself.

Sanford's conception is similar to that of C. W.
Leadbeater, a disciple of Madame Blavatsky, who wrote two
books that have been in print since 1902. The first is *Thought
Forms* and the second is titled *Man Visible and Invisible* in which
he explains,

> Occult chemistry shows us another and higher condition
> than the gaseous, into which all substances can be trans-
> muted and that condition is called etheric. . . . This higher
> matter is complex and with further subdivision we reach
> that realm of nature which occultists name the astral plane.
> . . . Further subdivision of the astral brings us to a third
> plane which in Theosophy we call mental. . . . These planes
> must not be imagined as lying above one another but rather
> as filling the same space and interpenetrating one another. The
> adult has usually over 90 percent of the matter of his astral
> and mental bodies within the periphery of his fleshly taber-
> nacle. [18]

Sanford expressed herself in a parallel fashion. She said
we are two bodies living together, the spiritual body interpenetrating the flesh.

> There is the one visible in the mirror, and there is the other
> one existing at a different vibration of energy, who is not
> visible in the mirror. . . . Is it not at least sensible to think
> that your spiritual body lives now? And if it lives now,
> where is it? Why, in you, in and around your other body, it's
> light permeating your physical body and emanating from
> your physical body and shining into the world around you.
> How do I know it is true? Because I have seen this light. [19]

Again her evidence was experiential, not biblical, and she
is admitting that she is clairvoyant. Ernest Holmes, founder
of Science of Mind, another New Thought cult, also speaks
of an actual spiritual body:

No doubt it will be proved there is something finer than the etheric. There is every reason to suppose that we have a body within a body and it is our belief we do have . . . we have a spiritual body and need not die to receive one.[20]

Why was it important for Sanford to believe there is an actual spiritual body? She needed a way to explain how her prayer of faith worked in healing. She questioned, "How could I believe my body was well and strong when the human part of me ached in every nerve?"[21] Her theology of a spiritual body made it possible for her to answer this question, to validate her theories of inner healing and give them a "Christian" veneer: if we have a divine body that is merged with the Holy Spirit, we have the attributes of God. One of these attributes she ascribed to God is perfection and therefore perfect health. How she used this idea in practice is best illustrated from her own words and from some actual experiences she related.

This spiritual body is part of me now, co-existing with the physical body. Therefore when I prayed for healing, I could accept the healing as already accomplished in the spiritual body, and so could know that it could be transferred to the physical body. Long before I received the gift of tongues, I received the understanding that the healing power of God moves through the spiritual body of man into his physical body.[22]

She related how she banged a heavy door on her finger and

it turned black immediately and the pain was excruciating. I said, "I have a spiritual body and in the spiritual body this finger is perfect." Immediately there appeared a tiny hole in the base of the fingernail and all the black blood oozed out.[23]

Sanford also suffered from severe headaches, and, as an attempt to heal herself of these she tried to 're-educate' her 'subconscious mind':

Therefore if we find ourselves thinking, 'One of my headaches is coming on,' we correct the thought. 'Whose headaches?' we say. 'God's light shines within me and God
doesn't have headaches!' And we rejoice in the Lord and give
thanks for His perfection that is being manifested within
us.[24]

The parallel to the healing experience which led Myrtle
Fillmore to found Unity along with her husband Charles, is
striking. From Myrtle's biography we read, "One Truth illumined the very depths of her soul: 'I am a child of God and
therefore I do not inherit sickness.'"[25] This same book quotes
Myrtle as saying, "The Truth came to me—a great revelation
showing me that I am a child of the one whole and perfect
mind created to express the health that God is."[26]

Unity teaches that we are actually children of God and
therefore part of His divine substance whereas the Bible
teaches we are adopted into His family when we acknowledge our sinful nature and accept Jesus as our Saviour (John
1:12; Rom. 8:15; Gal. 4:5; Eph. 1:5). To establish her system
of healing as unique Sanford needed to use different terminology from "New Thought" so she said spiritual body rather
than child of God to denote we are perfect as God is perfect. But the result is the same. Even so, *The Unity Guide to
Healing* expresses the same thoughts as Sanford,

> We are Spirit, of the Spirit of God, intrinsically perfect in
> God's perfectness. Jesus saw only the perfection of the spiri-
> tual body. God wills that we express His 'image' and 'like-
> ness' in which we were created. The will to be well comes
> from Him and the Spirit that does the healing work is not
> far from us.[27]

Chapter Nine:

Turning God On

Sanford's belief in a real spiritual body answered her question about how the prayer of faith worked to bring about healing. The second puzzle was how to access the power of God and transfer it to another person.

Sanford had a mechanistic view of God. She wrote many times that God is love. This seemed to be an abstract type of love for she never spoke of the tender, personal love God has for each of His redeemed children; a loving Father who knows what is best for His child. Instead, God's love is a matter of mechanically "learning to conform to His laws of faith and love. . . . God does nothing except by law. . . . God works immutably and inexorably by law."[1] This negates a personal relationship with God through Jesus Christ.

She repeatedly spoke of the physical laws which govern the earth and compared the power of God to such physical things as energy and electricity. Stating that everything in the universe is basically energy, she also wrote, "God is pure energy."[2] And in another book she wrote revealingly,

> "Ye are the light of the world." This is literally true. We are the electric light bulbs through whom the light of God reaches the world. Thus we are "part God." Knowing then that we are part of God, that His life within us is an active energy and that He works through the laws of our body, let us study to adjust and conform to those laws.[3]

A key concept of the New Age religions is their belief that God is energy and basic health is maintained only if there is a free flow of energy, or prana, or "god" through the body. This is the basis for acupuncture, reflexology, acupressure, therapeutic touch, and many other holistic health therapies. Thus she said, "the first step in seeking to produce results by any power is to contact that power. . . . The second step is to turn it on."[4] Similarly, *The Unity Guide to Healing* says, "Healing comes when the soul contacts God."[5]

So let us examine how she accessed this power, or energy, or "god," and how she turns it on. Her instructions were amazingly similar to Unity and Yoga and other New Age techniques in meditation. In the remainder of this chapter, I will compare Sanford's thinking on this point with these cults.

(1) Relaxation

The essential condition for contacting that power is to "Be still and know that I am God;" "to remind ourselves there is a source of life outside ourselves," even though "we may not know who God is or what God is, but we know that there is something that sustains this universe."[6]

She wanted us to contact this power not knowing if it is the power of Jehovah God or if it is a demonic spirit. Once, when working with a child who "didn't know anything about God", she talked to him about "there being something outside of yourself. After all, you didn't make this world. There's some kind of life outside of you." The boy replied, "Oh, sure. When you're scared enough you feel like there must be something." Sanford replied, "Well, then ask that Something to come into you."[7] Here Sanford was asking a boy who did not know Jesus as his Saviour to ask "Something" to come into him. Did she know what she was doing?

In her "more intense and advanced meditation," Sanford gave a specific technique for "being still" or "contacting that power." This involved relaxing and quieting the mind and getting the body comfortable:

First of all, subdue the energy of your body so that you can
forget it. . . . In order to receive God's life in the body, we
must first be able to forget the body so that we can quiet the
mind. . . . Sit comfortably. . . head at rest . . . hands folded in
the lap . . . the spine relaxed . . . so the chest can expand . . .
the breath is altered, becoming thin and light.[8]

She then described a hypnotic regime she called "more
than" auto suggestion for relaxing the body:

We bid our conscious minds be still. The control center we
call the subconscious mind conveys the order to the brain.
. . . Advise your nerves and muscles to be still. . . . Speak to
them kindly. . . in silence. . . . Say this to all your nerves
beginning with your head and carrying the same peaceful
thought down to your feet. . . . Imagine the peace of God
creeping down over your head, stilling its stream of consciousness . . . down over your hands and feet til limp . . .
down through your body so your heart beats lightly. . . .
Your breathing is light and easy.[9]

Then she allowed this power to enter:

So now that you are still, let your spirit enter into the spiritual kingdom. Imagine your spirit ascending through the
heavens and into the presence of God. . . . Some people are
also given to see visions or to have moments of cosmic
awareness. . . or to perceive the form or hear the voice of
Jesus.[10]

In her personal meditations, Sanford said she did not
have visions spontaneously for they "do not come unless we
open our awareness to receive them."[11] To open her awareness she imagined herself

wading into the ocean and floating on waves farther and
farther out . . . then I imagine my spiritual body as a shape
of light, arising out of my physical body and going higher
and higher in the air. . . . I attach my consciousness to this

spiritual body. . . . I am aware of earthly reality . . . but I see from far above that physical body like a tiny doll floating upon the waves. . . while I go higher and higher yet. . . and then I say, "Now Lord, this is as far as I can go. Open my eyes and show me what you want me to see."[12]

Unity also has the Prayer of Faith but the method of contacting or "unifying with" God is called "Silence." The following is from "A Drill in the Silence," a tract printed by Unity.

In practicing the silence you should always try to be relaxed in body and receptive in mind. . . . Let your whole body, every nerve, every muscle, every cell relax and let go. . . . Relax and let go until from the top of your head to the soles of your feet you are perfectly relaxed. "Be still and know that I am God." Know it. Know it now. . . . Repeat this silently over and over. . . . You are in the presence of God. . . . "I am the light of the world." Declare this. Then be still until you actually feel the light of the Spirit through you and over you, feel yourself immersed as in a sea of light, your whole being illumined, awake, exalted, the light of the world.[13]

New Age author Shaki Gawain writes similarly in her best selling book *Creative Visualization*,

Creative visualization involves understanding and aligning yourself with the natural principles that govern the workings of our universe . . . to have the experience of coming from source. Source means the supply of infinite love, wisdom and energy in the universe . . . or God or the universal mind. I like to think of contacting source as connecting with your higher self, the God-like being who dwells within you.[14]

To contact Source she advises,

Get in a comfortable position with your spine straight to help the energy to flow. . . in a quiet place. . . . Relax your body completely. Starting from your toes and moving up to your scalp, think of relaxing each muscle in turn. . . . Breathe deeply and slowly. . . to quiet inner mind chatter . . . silently practice doing affirmations.[15]

All meditation techniques are offshoots of yoga. Meditation is not prayer or meditation on the attributes of God as Christians would conduct themselves. Meditation involves an emptying of the mind as practiced by the gurus of India to allow "God" (Brahman, Vishnu, and Shiva) to enter in. For yoga means yoking the mind with "God." Yoga also teaches relaxation and how to monitor and slow the breathing so prana, or "God", or the universal life force, or energy, may flow freely through the body.

Sanford must have been accused of using yoga, since, later in her life, in an interesting defensive passage, she said, "So I began and continue at times to practice a way of mediation geared to a higher plane than this earth. This is not strange or far out. I do not practice deep breathing or contemplate my navel."[16]

Her decision to practice meditation "geared to a higher plane" followed a challenge by John Sandford: "I once wrote and urged him to close some of his spiritual centers or his psychic doors. Whereupon he wrote back and said, 'Why don't you try to open some of yours?'"[17]

(2) Imaging:

To turn the power on, the next step in the Prayer of Faith is to "make a picture in your mind of your body well."[18] Sanford's reasoning was, "I know that there actually is within man the power to create by thought: 'as he thinketh in his heart, so is he' (Proverbs 23:7)."[19] She justified this Theosophy teaching of thought-forms (discussed in a previous chapter) by using a part of a verse of Scripture completely out of context. Proverbs 23:6-7 reads, "Do not eat the bread of a miser, nor desire his delicacies; for as he thinks in his heart, so is he. 'Eat and drink!' he says to you, but his heart is not with you" (NKJV).

Using Proverbs 23:7, she went on to say,

> In other words we create by thought whether we want to do
> so or not. By negative thinking we open the way to illness,
> frustration, failure and disharmony. By positive thinking,
> i.e. faith, we open the way to health, creativity, success and
> harmony.[20]

> There is then a constructive power in positive thinking. It is
> not a substitute for religion. But it is one of God's laws and
> therefore unavoidable.[21]

Several times—four times in *Creation Waits* alone—she said,

> The thing on which we fasten our minds tends to come
> true. This is an inexorable law that cannot be altered. If we
> pray for healing of a friend and then continue to see that
> person lying on a bed of illness there is no power in the
> prayer. The picture that we see in our minds takes prece-
> dence over the prayer and renders it of no avail.[22]

Sanford used Fox's *Sermon on the Mount* as another "Bible"
in which he said,

> Remember that whatever the mind dwells upon will sooner
> or later come into your experience.... Now, a knowledge of
> the causative power of our (negative) thoughts will show us
> what the result must inevitably be. It must be to increase
> and multiply the trouble.... What really matters is thought.
> ... In the light of Scientific Christianity, thoughts literally
> are things.[23]

Again, this sounds very much like Unity's exaltation of
the mind to god-like status. Here are various comments from
Fillmore's *Unity Guide*:

> Mind is the one and only creative power.... When a person
> holds the thought that his body is pure, alive, and perfect
> no disease can touch him.... Thoughts are things.... Deny

negative inharmony of any kind. . . . The laws of mind are just as exact and undeviating as the laws of mathematics or music. . . . Allow Spirit to work thru you. Look at your chest: it breathes in the very breath of God's life; God is flowing through it to supply all your needs.[24]

(3) Affirmation

The final step was affirmation and speaking with authority—commanding God what He should do. This step of speaking with authority had three aspects. The *first* aspect was that of directing, as verified by Sanford:

> God's power is a real energy—a real force—a living force built into this world to do His will. . . . This energy is projected into this world by the word of power. . . . Any qualifying phrase, such as, "if it be thy will," decreases faith.[25]

At first she preferred using "so be it" as a command instead of as a statement of submission to God's will.

The *second* aspect of speaking with authority was the use of affirmations. Affirmations are positive statements used by those in New Thought cults. Sanford said, for example:

> The subconscious mind responds to suggestion. That is a law. When we see our faults and lacks and failures and repent of them, then we can go back to our positive thinking and say, "I am God's perfect child and His power is working within me toward life and health."[26]

> Thank you that your life is now coming into me and increasing life in my spirit and in my mind and in my body.[27]

Giving thanks was the *third* aspect of positive speaking. Sanford indicated that thanks was required before any healing would be accomplished: "And give thanks that this is being accomplished;"[28] "Yes you give thanks before you see the healing."[29]

The idea of positive speaking as a necessary technique in healing is a dominant thought in Unity, as well, as the following reveal:

> Speaking definite, positive words of assurance to oneself or to another has marvelous power to lift and transform, power to fill the body with a consciousness of the real living presence of God.[30]

The typical Unity affirmation also states,

> I am a child or manifestation of God, and every moment His life, love, wisdom, power flow into and through me. I am one with God, and am governed by His law.[31]

> Learn to give thanks in the realization you are already healed.[32]

New Age author Shakti Gawain seems to echo these same thoughts,

> Affirmations are one of the most important elements of creative visualization. An affirmation is a strong, positive statement that something is already so.[33]

Gawain's affirmations are short statements like "Divine light and love are flowing through me now" and "I am filled with divine light and creative energy."[34] Notice how similar these are to Sanford's affirmation cited above.

These are but representative quotations from Sanford and comparisons of those quotes with the Unity cult, Yoga, and the New Age movement. I would urge readers to make these comparisons themselves but keep in mind Sanford surrounds error with many Bible verses and some truth. Elizabeth Clare Prophet, leader of the Church Universal and Triumphant (CUT), one of the most occult of the New Age churches, has written several books, all of which contain more Bible verses than the average Christian book. We must beware of the 90% error mixed with 10% truth.

Chapter Ten:

Laying on of Hands

As described earlier, Hollis Colwell put his hands on the head of Sanford when he offered a prayer for healing from her depression. This was one of the first things she incorporated in her healing method. Laying on of hands sounds very spiritual and biblical until one examines what she was doing and the thinking behind it. Certainly her minister husband felt this was unorthodox.

> When I began, at the request of young mothers in my Bible class, to pray with laying on of hands for their children, Ted was much disturbed. Indeed, I found it best not to talk about my experiments in prayer, and for some four or five years they were hardly mentioned."[1]

Sanford acknowledged at least twice in her autobiography that churches considered her a heretic.[2] One conservative Christian periodical wrote they rejoiced that "Mrs. Sanford's sainted parents went to their reward before this book [*The Healing Light*] was published."

As I noted earlier, Sanford used James 5:14-15 to justify the name Prayer of Faith for her healing prayer but she also used it for giving credence to laying on of hands, after the manner of Hollis Colwell. However, she violated God's clear instructions in this verse when she used laying on of hands. First, the verse does not mention laying on of hands and second, she was not an elder.

Through her prayer of faith, Sanford seemed to have a method of contacting the god which she delineates variously as nature, a power, a force. Now she needed a method for transferring this power from herself to the one she was healing. This was done through laying on of hands: "I present first a way of becoming a receiving and transmitting center for love—healing by the laying on of hands."[3]

Christians need to know what she meant by this. First of all, the power was love: "Love is energy, not an emotion."[4] Since God is love (1 John 4:8) the power of God in Sanford's thinking was energy: *God = love = energy*. This depersonalizes God and His love for us as his adopted children. Another quote substantiates this: "The very chemicals contained in the body— the 'dust of the earth'—live by the breath of God by the primal energy, the original force that we call God."[5] This statement alone puts Sanford squarely in the New Age Movement.

She calls the Holy Spirit "a power, an energy, the water of life."[6] Yet the Bible teaches the Holy Spirit is a person who is our comforter and teacher (John 14:16-17,26; 15:7-15). She also called this power, light: "the light that heals is a real energy, the same creative energy from which all worlds were made; the original light of God."[7]

As a biblical illustration of laying on of hands she used the story of the barren Shunammite woman and Elisha who "connected himself with a current of God's energy and projected it by an act of faith into the body of the woman."[8] Or she would say it was the flow of love which she had already equated with energy/God. "In reading that book [*Oh Watchman*] you will see the reason and the value for touching the sick person. One then become[s] a connected channel, and therefore the power is transferred more readily, more quickly, and far, far more effectively."[9]

Several times in her books she described how the passage of this energy caused quivering of her hands.

When we pray for another with the laying on of hands, a power passes through us; a real energy; an actual radiation of a kind of light that cannot usually be seen by the eyes. This may cause our hands to quiver slightly as though a current of electricity were flowing through them, which in a way it is.[10]

She recounted how her "patients" often exclaimed that her hands felt hot from this energy. She even tried to explain that Jesus healed in this fashion:

> The most powerful healing method of all . . . [is] healing by the faith of someone else who acts as a receiving and transmitting center for the life of God. . . . It is the method Jesus used. . . . He interposed His whole being between God and the patient, so that He might be used as a channel for the life of the Father. He laid His hands upon blind eyes and deaf ears, that the currents of His own life vibration might flow through His spirit and mind and the nerves of His body into the bodies of the sick.[11]

Now that we have explained in her words what she meant by laying on of hands, I think we might say with confidence she was not only the "mother of Inner Healing", but she pioneered what is today called the Therapeutic Touch. We can also clearly see her ties to the New Age movement. The New Age movement popularized the Therapeutic Touch and has managed to have it taught in many nursing schools. Professor of Nursing, Dolores Krieger, has been an influential advocate of it through her classes at New York University and through her book, *The Therapeutic Touch*. She learned the procedure from Dora Kunz, president of Theosophy.

In earlier chapters we have shown the close ties Sanford had to Unity School of Christianity which has been described as "a saccharine version of Theosophy." It is not surprising, then, to regard Sanford's laying on of hands as an early version of Therapeutic Touch.

Confirmation of the similarity of New Age Therapeutic Touch and Sanford's Laying on of Hands is made from an actual workshop given at Red Rocks Community College,

September 17, 1988. I will attempt to condense Janet Mentgen's hour-long lesson (indented portions are my summary, taken from a transcribed tape):

> (1) Healing is an art not a science.

> (2) All healing is self-healing.

> (3) It creates what is called profound relaxation, getting towards zero muscle tone.

> (4) It's in this state of relaxation, when the healee is relaxed and the healer is centered [we need] to stop our mind from chattering. Centering is essential for the process.

In the New Age thinking, the word *centered* is used to denote a state of altered consciousness or self hypnosis. Remember that in Sanford's Prayer of Faith, the initial process is to induce relaxation or "silence" along with laying on of hands.

> (5) We know that in the human energy system, we are in constant flow, that energy must flow through our bodies for us to be healed. Anytime we have a congestion or slow down of that energy field or energy force, we begin to stop up or block—the seven energies—chakras.

> (6) So the concept is that our energy must come into our body, somehow it must flow through the body and it must come out of the body and that's the state of health. We believe the healer has an excess of this energy, called prana, the life force and the healee a deficit.

Remember that Sanford called this life force God. Hinduism agrees. This is also the basis for healing by acupuncture where needles are used to open the flow of this life force called chi.

> (7) Directing the modulating energy means that you can place your hands on or near the part that's having the problem

and direct energy from your palm into that place and begin to let the healing energies charge, like a battery. You feel warmth.

(8) With the ill person, we become like a channel.

Sanford also referred to being used as a channel, "In prayers for healing, especially with laying on of hands, this flow of power through the one who prays into the one who needs healing is tremendous. If I do not allow myself to be used as a channel, then nothing happens."[12]

Janet Mengen made the most revealing comment of all when she told her class that the Therapeutic Touch technique can be learned in two hours but it takes twelve hours to learn to stop the chattering of our mind, how to relax and get centered. This demonstrates that learning how to go deep within (self-hypnosis or centering) is more important than the nuances of the technique.

When we take Sanford's concept of God as energy, her repeated reference to herself as a channel of this energy into another person, and her methods of relaxation which simulates centering, we have an uncanny resemblance to the Therapeutic Touch.

Chapter Eleven:

Failure of the Prayer of Faith

Sanford started her ministry as a faith healer. As explained earlier, she claimed that Jesus Himself had given her sealed orders to eradicate physical illness. Her marching orders were John 14:22, "Verily, verily I say unto you, He that believeth on me, the works that I do shall he do also; and greater works than these shall he do; because I go to my Father." Since she believed the Church had failed miserably in this task, she consented to this mission.

Once, after she "healed" a young Jew, she claimed only two of the hundreds for whom she prayed failed to be healed.[1] These extravagant statistics were never verified; this is only hearsay evidence. But gradually her exuberance waned. She became physically drained and dispirited.[2] She came to realize "functional diseases are usually instantly healed" but "organic diseases such as cancer and arthritis, are naturally much more difficult than functional diseases."[3] She was admitting that disease which causes actual pathological changes in the body could not be healed by her Prayer of Faith. I give her credit for being honest.

She excused, however, the failure of her Prayer of Faith on the grounds of the fallibility of humans in our "present stage of spiritual development."[4] She admonished her followers to develop a spirit of discernment; to pray for the gift of wisdom.[5] Then they would not take the most difficult cases; they would know "when to stretch forth a hand and when to abstain."[6] Thus she screened carefully those she would treat. She would pick and choose. This would give her a better "cure" rate in her healing of the soul.

Another excuse for her failures in physical healing was the need for "arousing in the other person the faith to be healed."[7] She found this difficult to do. Innovative as always, she did found a way out. If they said they "didn't have any faith," she would reply, "That's all right. I can have faith for you."[8] She justified this procedure by saying Jesus did not demand faith of the children of Jarius and the children of the centurion or of the maniac of Gadara.[9]

She errs in three ways. First, Romans 10:17 says faith comes from hearing God's Word, not by someone having faith for them. And faith comes from the living Word, Jesus, who is "the author and finisher of our faith" (Heb. 12:2). Second, faith is a fruit of the Spirit (Gal. 5:22). And third, Jesus honored the faith of the parents, the centurion and Jairus, when He healed their children. The maniac fell down before Jesus and acknowledged He was the Son of God. Surely that is a demonstration of faith.

Sanford continued to be "a channel through whom others might receive healing,"[10] but her "own light had begun to grow dim. I was like a light whose oil was failing."[11] She and two of her friends became weary: "The Holy Spirit was not in me." They needed "some new outpouring of the direct power of God."[12] One friend, Marion, had a dream which pictured them laden down with other people's burdens. On the basis of this dream they prayed for strength. They received no strength. Then they prayed for healing of ills brought on by weariness. Again, they received no healing.[13]

Power of Tongues

After praying the Prayer of Faith for three days, they asked for guidance. A voice spoke "within all of them," telling them to pray for the Holy Ghost. This they did and "the power of the Spirit fell upon us immediately."[14] Sanford felt a deep and intense burning in the middle of her head like the "illumination" she received "when God's life" entered into her through the sunlight when she lay beside the "dancing waters of the lake"[15] in Vermont. God reveals himself to man in nature (Rom. 1:20) but is not a part of nature to be received through it. To believe that God can be received through sunlight or any other part of nature is pantheistic.

She did not mention this experience to her husband. "He did not like that kind of thing at all."[16] Within the year she also began to speak in tongues. After speaking in tongues in her private meditation time, "inspiration would come to me. Much of the latter part of *Behold Your God* was given to me in this way."[17] She also kept this a secret from her husband though not from others.

She spoke privately about tongues to those she deemed ready for this gift, most of whom were ministers. She instructed them to keep their gift of tongues a secret "for they would have been rejected by their congregations. . . . What I hope is that it [tongues] would spread through their churches so quietly and so gradually that when it comes out in public, your people will accept it."[18] The issue here is the deception by Sanford, not the validity of speaking in tongues.

Confession Time

Sanford recognized her Prayer of Faith did not work with true organic disease, so she looked to her experience with the Holy Spirit for the regeneration of her gift of healing. She prayed for more power and how to get it.[19] Her friend, Sister Leila Margaret of the Sisters of Saint Margaret Convent in Philadelphia, told her the confessional was the church's way of passing on power.[20] She sent Sanford to Father Weed for a life confession. For the first time she realized she needed forgiveness. She had given much thought to forgiving others but not of being forgiven herself because "I was not in the least conscious of sin."[21]

She made her first confession to Father Weed with a sense

of guilt that her Scottish Presbyterian ancestors were looking on.[22] Yet when she left, she was overwhelmed with vibrations of high ecstacy. This laid a foundation stone for her formulation of Inner Healing and Healing of Memories where the inner child is forgiven or comforted.

Some very acceptable passages on forgiveness and love in the Christian life follow these passages above. However, she interpreted confession as a way of transferring forgiveness through herself into another. She wrote, "I have found only one way of praying for another with real power while accomplishing an act of repentance. This is the ancient method of reparation wherein one makes available the sacrificial love of Christ for another by assuming his sins and doing penance for them."[23]

Did she really mean what she is saying? That she, in essence, is a sin-bearer for another? Christ alone bore our sin on the cross and paid the penalty (Is. 53; 1 Pet. 2:24). Christ took our sin upon himself, became sin, and made us righteous in the sight of God. As 2 Corinthians 5:21says: "For he hath made him to be sin for us, who knew no sin; that we might be made the righteousness of God in him."

Shifting Methods

What bearing does all this have on her healing methods? It shows they were in an ongoing state of transition. As before, her criteria for religious "truth" was, "Does it work?"[24] When something didn't work even when she claimed it was scriptural, she modified it. She found the prayer of faith had often failed to heal organic illness. She then added the dimension of confession of sin. But her re-thinking of God's thoughts led her in the wrong direction as evidenced by her defining sin as "sinful thought vibrations." She admitted in her autobiography she learned the term "thought vibrations" from Unity lecturer, Emmet Fox.

I believe that from a close scrutiny of her writings a person can deduce that Sanford confessed to "sinful thought vibrations." But did she ever confess she was born a sinner because of Adam's transgression? Did she ever confess she was in rebellion? Did she ever realize that when she rethought God's word, which she admitted, she was in reality disobeying it? The Unity School of Christianity teaches that sin is only an illusion. We have only inharmony, lack, and limitation. Positive thought vibrations will materialize good. Those who are not in tune with the Divine mind commit sins like murder, adultery, and stealing. Sanford, like those in Unity, probably did not consider herself a sinner because she had not made those mistakes.

It is no wonder, then, that the confessional brought only a temporary emotional high to Sanford. Her problem was being a "free spirit." Instead of surrendering the lordship of her life to Jesus, she relied on her own experiences and her "rethinking" of the Word of God.

We have seen how Sanford cast about for solutions to her discouraging dilemma. She had sealed orders from God but they seemed to remain sealed. Otherwise she would not have modified her methods. Her criterion for truth was "does it work?" She should have abandoned the prayer of faith when she realized it did not work, thereby fulfilling her own criterion for truth.

Chapter Twelve:

"Healing of the Soul Never Fails"

The prayer of faith failed. Sanford admitted it worked only for functional illness not organic, physiological disease. After she had admitted this, she took the next logical step: "Of recent years my interest has veered away from healing of the body and has been guided almost entirely into this deeper area; the healing of the soul,"[1] and interestingly enough, "the healing of the soul never fails."[2] She was making the same claims for inner healing (healing of the soul) that she formerly made for her prayer of faith. This is interesting in the light of her self-admitted failure with her "command" or faith prayer. She then launched into a mixture of New Thought/occult and Jungian depth psychology and emerged with Inner Healing/Healing of Memories and the Inner Child.

I will examine the New Thought/occult aspect of her healing of the soul and then peruse how Jung's influence affected her writings about the soul.

In the previous chapters on the prayer of faith, I have pointed out that a key to understanding Sanford's rationale for the way it worked was her unbiblical idea that every person has a spiritual body as real as their physical body.

The spiritual body is essential to inner healing and such offshoots as "prayer of healing at a distance" which she also called intercession. Sanford always laid hands on the person who came to her for healing and prayer. She had to have physical contact if she was to be the channel for transference

of God's power into the patient. This presented a problem
for Sanford. How could she be effectual when she was physically separated from the person, sometimes by thousands of
miles? She wrote, "I was now feeling the sweep of power
through me more and more when I laid hands on someone
to pray, but in praying from a distance, nothing happened.
There was some key I was not turning."[3]

The key that she was not turning was the spiritual body:
"The spirit is apparently able to travel quite a distance from
the [physical] body and still maintain a connection with our
beings. Some call this ability of the spirit 'astral traveling.'"[4]
She was referring to a spiritual body. She made this clear by
stating, "But that it does travel and that God does work
through my spiritual body . . . becomes more and more apparent."[5] By her admission to astral traveling, Sanford revealed
explicit connections to the occult.

Healing at a Distance

This solved her dilemma. The prayer of faith would work
at a distance now that her spiritual body could be used as the
channel for power to be transferred to the person for whom
she prayed. She didn't need to be there physically. She illustrated this "truth" by telling those who had no success with
their prayers to read one of her prayers out loud when they
were alone. They were to pretend they were hearing the words
from her lips—"not mine as a human being, but mine as a
spiritual being whose spiritual body God can use as a trained
channel for the healing of the soul."[6]

In essence, she was saying that when she could not be
with a person physically, her spiritual body could travel to be
with that person to be used as a channel by God. This sounds
very much like a type of spiritual mediumship. Sanford repeated over and over in her books the idea of being a channel through which God can work,

> It is only the channeling of a flow of energy from God's
> being through man's being . . . via the conscious and sub-

conscious mind of that man. The message [Logos] is sent from the Spirit of God in a mysterious way through the spirit, mind and body of the one who prays into the body, mind and spirit of the patient.[7]

This quote from Sanford reveals a clear similarity to the occult teachings of Theosophy, as they appear in the book *Thought Forms,*

On every plane our Logos pours forth His light, His power. ... There are conditions under which the grace and strength peculiar to a higher plane may be brought down to a lower one... when a special channel is opened... by the effort of man. The result of the descent of divine life is a strengthening of the make or the channel, and the spreading around him of a beneficent influence. This has been called an answer to prayer.[8]

Why did Sanford seem compelled to have these elaborate mechanisms for her various types of prayer? Because her prayers were basically "do it yourself," tipping her hat to God but giving Him a minor role. She did not need to be omnipresent in her spiritual body for God is omnipresent. Therefore, we pray to God and He hears us. God hears and God answers; God acts.

But Sanford apparently believed the prayer must be sent to the person for which they prayed, not to God: "so they prayed and sent the words of forgiveness toward the man at a distance."[9] Statements such as this, made throughout her books show continuing similarity between her theology and the occult. Theosophy, for example, teaches it also. Annie Bessant, successor to Madame Blavatsky, explained it as "A thought of love and desire to protect, directed strongly toward some beloved object, creates a form which goes to a person thought of, and remains in his aura as a shielding and protecting agent.... Thus we may create and maintain veritable guardian angels around those we love."[10] Sanford said nearly the same thing: "Our spirits are able to respond to the call of prayer or to the need of some loved one to go and minister to them without the awareness of the conscious mind."[11]

Once again the occultic teaching of thought forms was the basis for this concept, not Scripture. The foreword of Theosophy's book *Thought Forms* states, "It has been demonstrated that thought can traverse great distances, can affect people and objects, and is indeed a tangible factor in the invisible world around us." The cover further describes the authors, Annie Besant and C. W. Leadbeater, as endowed with "unusual clairvoyant ability,"[12] investigators of man's invisible nature and powers.

A practical example of Sanford's use of thought forms was to influence her children by "remote control." She made no mention of prayer to God. Instead she described it thus when she heard her children quarreling: "After a few months practice . . . I had only to make in my mind the image of a child at peace and project it into reality by the word of faith."[13]

Concerning the ability of the spirit to leave the body, Sanford also taught, "the spirit can, by stretching the silver cord that links it to the body (Eccl. 12:6), reach the heavenly kingdom while we sleep and return to us refreshed and inspired with new knowledge."[14] The idea that the spirit is floating around outside the body linked by a silver cord is another occult concept. This is how they explain the ability of the spirit body to travel away from the physical body. Here is another blatant example of the way Sanford had a pre-conceived conclusion and threw in a Bible verse to try to justify it. The Bible teaches that the spirit stays in our body and it leaves only at death. If we are Christian, our spirit leaves us to be present with the Lord (2 Cor. 5:5-8). Ecclesiastes 12:7 confirms this also.

With her idea of the silver cord, she tried to justify the many excursions into heaven she had while sleeping or during her meditations. Sprinkled throughout her books she described the call to "Come up hither!" In her last book, *Creation Waits*, she wrote that she has been many times in the New Jerusalem, "escaping lightly from the bonds of my human being, and to live for awhile in the spirit in one of the mansions of heaven."[15]

Other Spiritual Powers

Because of Sanford's belief in the ability of our spirit to leave our body and travel, she claimed it explained "a number of extra-sensory gifts: prophecy or pre-cognition, discernment of spirits, clairaudience, clairvoyance: all of these being the natural results of developing and expanding of spiritual powers."[16]

The developing of the spiritual powers produced a "mysterious connection between the unconscious being of one person and the deep mind of another." This connection created the possibility "that the unconscious mind may make rapport with the unconscious mind of someone living anywhere upon this earth or someone who has lived before or someone who will live in the future or even of someone from heaven."[17]

Sanford emphasized connecting with someone who had lived long ago and she also explained the mechanism of ESP and communicating with the dead.

> We know that we have within us another mind than the conscious, and that this unconscious mind is not disconnected from life but is connected within the mind of the race: the collective unconscious. Therefore we can "pick up" thoughts and impressions from another life or from life outside ourselves or from the memories of the race.[18]

Not only is ESP an occult activity, but in these passages Sanford was explaining how we have the ability to communicate with the dead. This is expressly forbidden in Scripture (Lev. 20:27; Deut. 18:11); it was the cause of Saul's death (1 Chron. 10:13).

Sanford tried to give credence to ESP by citing as ex-

amples the direct revelations from God contained in the four
books of the Major Prophets. Sanford threw up a smoke
screen by saying that modern man explores these mysteries
through the psychic "yet they are a natural and integral part
of the life of the spirit, and if the spirit of man is energized
by the Holy Spirit of God, these super-sensory gifts come to
one in a more useable fashion than can ever be obtained by
mere psychic research."[19]

She explained ESP by Jung's theory of the unconscious
and the collective conscious. Then she tried to make Jung's
non-Christian philosophy palatable by invoking the Holy Spirit
as part of the process:

> The actual deep therapy of the Holy Spirit is done not by us
> at all but by Him. And it is done through the union of two
> souls [the therapist and the patient]. It is not strange that
> we find ourselves knowing matters about a person's past no
> one has ever told us. While the work is done by the Holy
> Spirit, the possibility of such instinctive knowing is already
> potentially within our natures. "Thought transference" it is
> called; the passage of thoughts from unconscious to un-
> conscious.[20]

In previous chapters we have discussed her occultic beliefs such as thought forms, seances, and her endorsement of
Emmet Fox, premier lecturer for New Thought. In this chapter we have shown the role her unbiblical spiritual body played
in healing of the soul. When we add to this her endorsement
of ESP and communicating with the dead, even though she
tried to cover it with the patina of Christian words, I think
we need to wonder about her source of knowledge.

Chapter Thirteen:

Inner Healing and Memories

What is Inner Healing? Agnes Sanford never gave a real definition, but since she equated the Soul with the unconscious or deep mind, this gives us a start. Inner Healing is healing of the unconscious or subconscious through healing-counseling sessions which incorporate some of the mechanisms used for physical healing, such as meditation-visualization.

In *Healing Light,* she explained her Prayer of Faith and the role of positive thought-forms in healing of the body. She mentioned the subconscious only three times in the context of "teaching ourselves a new thought-habit; re-educate the subconscious mind." She gave a few glimpses of future emphasis on the soul when she wrote about thought-habits of hate and other "sinful thought vibrations."

In her following books, she developed the role of the unconscious in healing of the deep mind. The climax came in *Healing Gifts of the Spirit,* which was written after she embraced speaking in tongues. There she admitted faith healing of the body can fail, but "healing of the soul never fails."[1]

If she was claiming her Inner Healing never fails, this was such a sweeping claim it boggles the mind. Was she speaking about the peace with God that comes with repentance for sin and accepting Jesus as Lord and Saviour? This never fails (Rom. 5:1). Or was she speaking of the peace of God which is part of sanctification? This can fail, for even Paul struggled against his "old nature" (Rom. 7:15-24). Although we are declared righteous when we accept Jesus as Savior, complete sanctification becomes a reality only when we go home to be with the Lord.

Three times in *Healing Gifts of the Spirit* alone, Sanford declared that healing of the soul never fails: "Is not the healing of the soul the very purpose of His holy sacrifice on Calvary?"[2] She made this pronouncement based on her odd view of sin and the soul. I pointed out earlier that Sanford wrote repeatedly of her definition of sin as "sinful thought vibrations." She identified the soul as the deep mind of unconsciousness. Putting these two concepts together she said redemption meant healing of the memories (or deep mind or unconscious) from our sinful thought vibrations.

Why does the quotation above distress me? She said Jesus died on Calvary not to reconcile sinners to God, but to heal the soul. Yet Colossians 1:19-22 tells us that Christ's death was to reconcile sinful man to God. Without Jesus dying as a sinless substitute for basic sin, we would still be lost and undone. We would remain spiritually dead. We would spend eternity in separation from God.

Sanford struggled with her misunderstanding of redemption and positional sanctification as contrasted with experiential and ultimate sanctification. When we are redeemed by the shed blood of Jesus we are also cleansed, forgiven, and declared righteous sons of God. This is called positional sanctification and should inspire us to holy living[3] while "ultimate sanctification is related to our final perfection, and will be ours in the glory."[4]

Sanford also admitted she was puzzled by the need for the cross.

> I had been taught all my life: that Jesus forgives sins. This tenet of theology had become increasingly puzzling to me as I learned more of the power of faith. For the question was, if the power of right thinking could establish in us the thing we affirm, then why was the Cross necessary?[5]

Centrality of the Unconscious

Throughout her books Sanford designated the heart as the unconscious. She was a self-acknowledged student of New Thought teacher, Emmet Fox, and she may have derived this from him. He wrote, "The word heart in the Bible usually means that of man's mentality which modern psychology knows under the name of the subconscious mind."[6] Using this definition, Mark 7:20-21 would read: "And he said, That which cometh out of man, that defileth the man. For from within, out of the *unconscious* of men, proceed evil thoughts, adulteries, fornication, murders."

When Jesus said out of the heart come the sins of evil thought, adultery, fornication, murder he was giving the diagnosis. But I disagree with Sanford about the cure. The Bible does not teach that the cure comes from within ourselves.

Just as we cannot save ourselves, we cannot sanctify ourselves. Our cure comes from God. Sanford proclaimed that she followed only "what Jesus Himself said" and "paid no attention to the Bible nor St. Paul"[7] though later on she did add the Ten Commandments as a yardstick.

To understand why Sanford went to the inner self for healing, we must refer back to the impact that New Thought and other cults had on her. The foundation of Inner Healing is her understanding of the nature of God. New Age/New Thought holds to the pantheistic view that God is in and a part of everything that exists. As I have already shown, Sanford was pantheistic. One outgrowth of this belief is that we are part of God, part of the divine order. Though this is also New Age/New Thought, they express it in more subtle ways. They speak of finding "self" meaning that we are god but we need to believe it; raise our consciousness high enough to experience it. If we are god, where else would we go but into our inner self for healing, especially healing of the soul? Sanford never boldly stated that we are divine, but she made it implicit throughout her books.

Gospel of Healing

Sanford brought her "Gospel of Healing"[8] to pastors who attended her Schools of Pastoral Care. She found a more extensive audience when Glen Clark of Camps Farthest Out published her first books. Though her theology was initially considered heresy, it was eventually accepted by many churches when she switched the emphasis from physical healing to healing of the soul—deep mind—unconscious. She retained all of the teaching which had its roots in New Thought, however. She retained the Unity-like prayer of faith and the Theosophy-like laying on of hands. Sanford also kept the same step-by-step process of yoga-like relaxation, controlled breathing, centering, visualization and silence (meditation) for contacting God.

The practical part of going within seemed to have its beginnings when she embraced the confessional on the advice of two Roman Catholic sisters. It may also have been because of her knowledge of Jungian psychology. Jung wrote, "The first beginnings of all analytical treatment are to be found it its prototype, the confessional."[9]

Prior to going to confession she admitted she had never been conscious of sin.[10] After Father Weed gave her a "life confession," she went to him monthly and made "my small confessions. . . they were not sensational." She continued this self-examination for things she could remember committing during that month. But "there were still areas needing healing that his monthly confession did not touch."[11]

It was at this point, according to her autobiography, she learned of the areas her confession did not touch. A physician she had met at Camps Farthest Out pointed out to her "there was something in her memories" causing her nervousness. Thus, Healing of Memories became the final point of Sanford's theology in her long search for physical and soul healing.

Healing of Memories

At long last Sanford came to the culmination of her belief system: Healing of Memories. She received her inspiration from a physician. Or was it "directly from God?"[12] Or was it from within herself? She gave three different accounts. She equated her guidance with intuition and "hunches."[13]

She changed the main focus of attention from positive thought vibrations, commanding God through her faith prayer, laying on of hands, to memories (the unconscious).

Let us begin with a description of the theory behind healing of memories in Sanford's own words.

> Something is troubling the deep mind. . . some old unpleasant memory. . . . What are these 'roots of bitterness' and how can they be drawn out of us? . . . We are apt to drag chains fastened upon our souls so long ago that we do not even know what they are. . . burdens put upon our souls when we were too little to be responsible? . . . Yet there is hope, because God is involved with time, . . seeing our need He incarnated Himself and became man, thus entering into the collective unconscious of the race. . . . Jesus is our time-traveler, . . . out of timelessness into our time, on purpose to transcend time in each of us, entering the subconscious and finding His way through past years to every buried memory in order to touch it with His healing power and set us free. I ask Jesus to enter into him, and go back through time and heal the memories of fear and resentment—even those he had forgotten . . . then I ask Jesus to walk into the past—back though their memories . . . and set them free. . . . For this 'healing of the memories' is redemption. This is the saving of the soul.[14]

I do not disagree that memories are a reality and that every person has memories. Sanford's Healing of Memories does not deal with all memories, however. It deals only with painful memories. The lives of Paul and David illustrate what our attitude toward painful memories should be. Paul had relentlessly persecuted Christians before his conversion. What graphic memories could have haunted him. Yet in Philippians

3:13-14 he makes this magnificent statement, "But this one thing I do, forgetting those things which are behind, and reaching forth unto those things which are before, I press toward the mark for the prize of the high calling of God in Christ Jesus."

David became a hunted fugitive due to the malevolent hatred of Saul towards him. David went to Saul for reconciliation and also refrained from killing him when he had the opportunity. Then David looked to God for comfort and deliverance instead of exorcising painful memories.

If the Holy Spirit brings to our mind a memory of some wrong we have committed we should be obedient to Jesus' commands. Throughout the New Testament we are commanded to go to the person we have wronged or has wronged us. In obedience to the Word we should go to others to be reconciled to them (Matt. 5:23-24). This is vastly different from going through an hypnotic procedure to reach an inner child for comfort and forgiveness over true/untrue hurts.

God heals painful memories by enabling us to forget them. God has shown us this through His example of forgiving the sinner when he repents (1 John 1:9), and His example of forgetting the sins (Heb. 8:12; 10:17). No trial or memory is unique to God. He has given us a remedy which will enable us to bear the trial, or hurt, or distress. God is all sufficient. The Bible gives insight into human nature. God addresses all situations involving emotions, personalities, temptations and trials through the stories of the saints and sinners, in the Psalms and Proverbs. 1 Corinthians 10:13 comforts us in this, "There hath no temptation [trial] taken you but such is common to man: but God is faithful, who will not suffer you to be tempted above that which you are able; but will with the temptation also make a way of escape, that you may be able to bear it."

The disagreement with Sanford is her peculiar syncretism of memories with healing. She tried to give it credibility from the Bible. She did this in two ways. First, by her (occultic) concept that humans possess a divine-spiritual body which can travel outside the body.

Second, she had an unusual belief about Jesus and our spiritual bodies traveling through time. I do not contest the fact that God is not constrained by time and space. But Sanford specifically states Jesus is our "time traveler."[15] Although she did not mention the spiritual body of Jesus she implied this when she wrote that the "idea of the spiritual body and the physical body, and of the Spirit of God permeating the spiritual body, is the very foundation stone of the whole Bible, . . . the reality of the spiritual body that interpenetrates the physical body and the spiritual world in which we really live."[16]

According to Sanford, not only does Jesus travel through time, He takes us with Him. "The Lord will walk back with you into the memories of the past so they will be healed."[17] And "Imagine Him walking back with you through time and finding the small person who was agonized and torn apart."[18]

I acknowledge God is omnipresent and knows the past, present and future. But it is radically different to believe Jesus travels through time today in his spiritual body when the Bible says Jesus is in Heaven where He is our High Priest and Advocate before our Father (Heb. 7-9).

The disciples actually saw Jesus in His glorious body after His resurrection. Would not Christians actually see Him in His glorified body today, not just visualize Him in their mind, if He was time-traveling for us? Jesus did appear and disappear miraculously during the time between His resurrection and ascension into heaven. But Jesus is not traveling or appearing and disappearing now. Instead, the Scriptures tell us where He is: "So then after the Lord had spoken unto them, he was received up into heaven and sat on the *right hand of God*" (Mark 16:19, emphasis mine). And He continues to sit at the right hand of God (Ps. 110:1; Heb. 10:12).

Step by Step

Sanford gave the most comprehensive exposition of her counseling in *The Healing Gifts of the Spirit*, where she outlined the seven steps of her method. Her disciples still use this method, with their individual variations, which differ little from her basic strategy:

1. *Jesus enters the collective unconscious to redeem memories.* She explained that healing of memories is redemption for which Jesus entered into the "collective unconscious"; humans are bound by time so Jesus is our "Time Traveler"; "the Lord will walk back with you into the memories of the past so that they will be healed."

2. *Know the patient's childhood.* She inquired about their childhood. If a patient said they had a very happy childhood, she asked three basic questions:
a. When did you start being unhappy?
b. Why were you so unhappy?
c. What happened that made you feel that nobody loved you?

3. *Wait for them to get over fears and embarrassments.* Knowing they were "holding something back out of fear or embarrassment," she waited for the rest to come forth.

4. *Clear the mind.* She had the patient relax, meditate (empty the mind) as she did with her prayer of faith. She laid her hands on them to "transfer the love of Christ into them."

5. *See Jesus interacting with their inner child.* She prayed and had the patient use their creative imagination to visualize Jesus taking them back through time to the scene during their childhood when they were hurt and felt unloved, relive the emotions involved.

6. *Pray for healing, even for times before birth.* She prayed for the Lord to "go back through all the rooms of this memory-house . . . see if there be any dirty and broken things. . . take them completely away . . . go back even to the nursery in this memory house . . . back to the hour of birth . . . even

before birth if the soul was shadowed by this human life and was darkened by the fears and sorrows of the human parents."[19]

7. *See yourself as God meant you to be.* "Power of visioning; in the healing of memories one must firmly hold in the imagination the picture of this person as God meant him to be, seeing though the human aberrations and perversions . . . and turn in the imagination the dark and awful shadows of his nature into shining virtues and sources of power. This is redemption."[20]

Secular psychologists call the healing of memories depth psychology, and Sanford admitted that her healing of the deep mind is also depth psychology. She wrote about a psychiatrist she was teaching, who, "Listening in amazement, grew white as a sheet and gasped, 'But that is depth psychology!' Of course it is!"[21]

Sanford was teaching depth therapy by the Holy Spirit, "done through the union of two souls. It is not strange that we find ourselves knowing matters about a person's past that no one has ever told us. 'Thought transference' it is called; the passing of thoughts from unconscious [of one person] to unconscious [of another person]."[22]

Problems with Memory Healing

Specific criticisms of healing of memories involve three areas. First, I have covered extensively two topics in previous chapters which relate to New Thought/New Age. These are the yoga-like techniques for contacting God—relaxing, controlled breathing and meditation, which she carried over from her prayer of faith—and visualization.

Second, I have given biblical reasons why Jesus does not travel through time to heal the inner child and why healing of memories is not redemption.

Third, on a practical level, I am appalled at her counseling. Not only did she ask leading questions of those who admit to an unhappy childhood, she planted the seed of suggestion and doubt in the mind of those who had a happy childhood. I have found that those who have written books on *Healing of Memories* (David Seamonds) and *Transformation of the Inner Man* (John and Paula Sandford) do the same thing—working hard through suggestion until the patient finally dredged up some hurt from his past.

She gave a blatant example of this in *The Healing Touch*. But it had a different twist to it. She wrote about a Jewess who had been tormented and driven out of Germany because of her race. She had forgiven her tormentors but "in spite of prayer there was sorrow in her mind." Sanford thought it must be "the little child in her who could not throw stones at those who threw stones at her because there were so many." She could only hide deep in her memories the feelings of resentment and fear when her parents were taken off to a concentration camp.

Sanford tried to get the woman to recall these memories she must have had.

> We tried to bring them to her mind, and had failed. They were buried so deep that she was completely unaware of their existence. So I thought, "I will repent of them in her name." I will say to Jesus Christ, "Let the grown woman free, for I will take the responsibility for her sins of fear and hate. Since she cannot see them herself to repent of them herself, I will repent of them in her name and so open the door for the forgiveness of Jesus Christ."[23]

If the person being counseled prayed, Sanford didn't hesitate to break into their prayer to guide and mould their thinking and sometimes she even wrote out the prayer for them to pray.[24]

Another serious flaw in her counseling occurred when her "patient" might reveal "the worst thing he can possible tell about himself." Sometimes there was a conscious confession of sins, but most often the person does not even think of his conversation as a confession. In these cases I often say afterwords, "But, you know that is not your real self at all." And I describe the picture of the real self that God has helped me to work out of my creative imagination. . . . This is often amazing, overwhelming, and tremendously releasing. . . that another human being could see him as a saint of God! . . . Seeing it one draws it forth . . . this is agape, or the love of God made human.[25]

In this passage she had been using homosexuality as an example. She equated revealing sin to a counselor as a confession of sin. The remedy she gave was not confessing the sin to God and asking forgiveness. Her remedy was to tell him he is a saint of God. If being told this causes some change, it would be self-reformation and not biblical regeneration.

Sanford was rather casual about the eternal destination of those who sought her help. She seemed to assume everyone was a Christian.

The first duty of a Christian counselor or healer is to determine if the person seeking help is a true believer. If they aren't, an attempt should be made to lead them to Christ for this is their primary problem. The fruits of the Spirit—love, joy, peace, longsuffering, gentleness, goodness, faith, meekness, temperance—are given to those who walk in the Spirit. But first they must have the Spirit through accepting Jesus as Saviour and Lord.

Chapter Fourteen:

The Inner Child

The importance of the inner child to inner healing cannot be overemphasized. This was not derived from the Bible, but was taken whole cloth from C. G. Jung.

Reclaiming the Inner Child is a 300-page compendium of articles by contemporary psychiatrists and Jungian therapists. The editor, Jeremiah Abrams, traces the evolving concept of the Inner Child from the "mystical traditions" of the child-god Hermes, the alchemist Philosopher's Child, the Hindu child Krishna, to the depth psychologies of Freud, Adler, Jung, Reich and Reik.

Abrams says, "The concept emerges in the serious and popular psychological literature of the 1960s, most notably in the works of the pre-eminent Swiss psychiatrist C. G. Jung (The Psychology of the Child Archetype, 1959 American edition)" and "In the past three decades the phenomenon of the inner child has risen in prominence largely because of a growing interest in Jungian depth psychology."[1] American psychiatrist W. Hugh Missildine brought the inner child into 'pop' self-help psychology with his book, *Your Inner Child of the Past*.

Unfortunately, many Christians have been seduced through atheistic Jungian psychology of the inner child. Jung predicted this in the 1930s when he wrote, "The wave of interest in psychology which is sweeping over the Protestant countries of Europe is far from receding. It is coincident with the general exodus from the Church. Quoting a Protestant minister,

I may say: 'Nowadays people go to a psychotherapist rather than to a clergyman.'"[2]

Jung, an agnostic, called himself a Protestant. Perhaps he did this to distinguish himself from the original psychoanalysts who were Jews. His father and maternal grandfather were Protestant ministers in Switzerland. His grandfather

> had visions and conversed with the world of the spirits, and in his study he had a special chair reserved for the spirit of his deceased first wife, who visited him every week. His grandmother was said to possess the gift of second sight, and several of her family to have parapsychological abilities.[3]

Jung said his mother showed occult powers and his pastor father had religious doubts.[4]

Jung emphasized in his autobiography his inner life during his teenage years, his fantasies, dreams, intuitions and even memories of a previous life. A natural result was that Jung underwent a religious crisis between his fifteenth and eighteenth years marked by tedious, sterile discussions with his father. He came out of this crisis an agnostic which was expressed by his favorite statement, "I cannot believe in what I do not know, and what I know I need not believe in."

Thus, we should not be surprised that Jung "devoured whatever he could find written on spiritism and parapsychology . . . was passionately interested in such authors as Swedenborg, Mesmer and Schopenhauer . . . Jung relates his discovery of Nietzsche was a major event of this period."[5] When he was twenty-three years old he joined a group performing spiritistic experiments with a young medium, his cousin, Helen Preiswerk. These experiments formed the basis for his medical dissertation in 1902.[6]

The influence that Jung had on Sanford is apparent by her many references to him and her use of his terminology and concepts of the collective unconscious and archetype and dreams. Her pastor Morton Kelsey and her son John, are avowed Jungian counselors especially using dream therapy.

Jungian Problems

The basic argument against healing of memories of the inner child is against its foundation: Jungian psychology. Christians are to have the mind of Christ (1 Cor. 2:16) not the carnal mind affected by occultic influences "because the carnal mind is enmity against God: for it is not subject to the law of God, neither indeed can be" (Rom. 8:7). Christians live in a secular world and enjoy the benefits of things invented by non-Christians. But when it comes to our minds and spirits, we must be separate from the world.

What exactly is this "inner child?" Healing of memories postulates that within all of us lives a second person or personality, a fragile child who has been hurt unjustly. But the memories of these hurts have been forgotten. Healthy spirit life is thought to depend on bringing these memories to light so the inner child can be forgiven for being hurt and then be comforted. Helping to recall these memories is the counseling aspect of healing of memories.

In this so-called Christian counseling, once these memories had been liberated from the unconscious, the counselor would usually pray. During the prayer the couselor would instruct you to relax your body, regulate your breathing, go deep within yourself, and quiet your mind. Then you are told to visualize yourself, usually standing by a stream in a beautiful pastoral scene. Next you visualize a man in a shimmering white robe walking toward you, holding a small child by the hand. You recognize the child as yourself. When you look into the man's face you realize it is the face of Jesus.

Jesus introduces you to your inner child and asks you to receive the little child in His name, to welcome it into your heart, to love this child free from your defense mechanisms. You are to ask this inner child for forgiveness for rejecting and hurting it. Jesus puts His arms about the child and loves and comforts it. Or you may visualize Jesus tenderly taking your inner child onto His lap. This is a reasonable composite of what Sanford and her followers do with visualization of the inner child, though they may use variations on the scenario I have just painted.

Sanford based her justification for literally going back through time and visualizing the inner child and Jesus mainly on her own interpretation of Jung's ideas of inner healing. She does attempt to bring in the Bible by making a brief reference to Jesus blessing the children.

However, her only other attempt to square this with Scripture is a belabored use of 1 Peter 3:19-20, "By which also he went and preached unto the spirits in prison; which sometimes were disobedient, when once the longsuffering of God waited in the days of Noah, while the ark was a preparing, wherein few, that is eight souls were saved by water." She wrote about the gifts of the Spirit in this revealing quote,

> We are learning to see with the eye of the spirit as well as with the physical eye. . . . In the larger world, the heavenly kingdom, time is telescoped. . . . When it has a purpose, God allows us to see into the accumulated thought vibrations of the ages, and feel the feelings and think the thoughts of someone who lived long ago. . . we do not need to live again and again in time, for we live presently in all time if we did but know it. . . . Can we send our prayer power back through time? Is this what Jesus did when He descended into hell and prayed for the spirits who were in prison in the time of Noah? (1 Peter 3:19-20) Is this the explanation of the prayer of the healing of memories?[7]

More Problems

How desperate Sanford must have been for some verses to try to justify healing of memories. It also reveals her *modus operandi*: develop a theory, then try to fit Scripture to that theory, giving the verses a "deeper" meaning than they contain. Sometimes Christians become jaded, start looking for "fresh insights" into Scripture, often listening to the so-called deeper "spiritual" interpretation offered by the cults.

When we look at the whole Scripture, we see that Jesus did not go back through time or send His prayer power back through time to the days of Noah as Sanford says. Jesus descended into Sheol, the waiting place of the dead and preached to those who had been waiting there since the time of Noah. He went there during a definite time frame, between his death and resurrection.

As Christians, what are we to think of the inner child and visualizing Jesus? J. I. Packer in his book, *Knowing God*, makes a compelling argument against visualizing God in our mind. He bases this on the second commandment because the first commandment already has forbidden worshipping idols ("having other Gods before me"). The second commandment says, "Thou shalt not make unto thee any graven image, or any likeness of any thing that is in heaven above, or that is in earth beneath, or that is in the water under the earth: thou shalt not bow down thyself to them, nor serve them: for I the Lord thy God am a jealous God" (Ex. 20:4).

Historically, Protestants have made the stand that idolatry is not the worship of false gods only, but also the worship of any person of the Triune God by use of images. Packer points out that mental images of God affect our thoughts of God in two important ways.

First, "They dishonor God, for they obscure His glory. 'A true image of God is not found in all the world. To devise any image of God is impious; because by this corruption His majesty is adulterated, and He is figured to be other than He is,' wrote John Calvin."[8] So then the commandment is saying pictures, and visualization of Jesus as a man, although He was and remains a man, is idolatry because our conceptions of man, even the most ideal man, are impure by God's standards. God is not man and though we are made in His image, we are not to conceive of Him in man's impurity. If God, in His wisdom, knew it was an essential part of worship for us to have a representation of Jesus, He would have provided it. Perhaps this is why no paintings or statues were made of Jesus during His incarnation.

Second, Packer says, "Images mislead men. They convey false ideas about God. The very inadequacy with which they represent Him perverts our thoughts of Him, and plants in

our minds errors of all sorts about His character and will."[9]
We see this in the actions of the Israelites. They conceived a
symbol of the might and strength of God and then Aaron
made a golden calf for them to worship. This false image led
to wild debauchery and the judgement of God upon them.

Our concept of God will be the God we worship,
whether it is the God revealed in the Bible or not. Some healing of memories counselors encourage their patients to visualize Jesus and the inner child daily until they are "healed"
spiritually. If we habitually focus our thoughts on an image
of Jesus we come to think of Him and pray to Him as we
imagine Him. Packer says, "Thus you will in this sense 'bow
down and worship' your image; and to the extent to which
the image fails to tell the truth about God, to that extent you
will fail to worship God in truth. That is why God forbids
you and me to make use of images in our worship."[10]

We find God through His attributes, character and promises which we find in the Scriptures. The second commandment compels us to take our thoughts of God from His Word,
not from other sources. Packer says, "The mind that takes up
images is a mind that has not yet learned to love and attend to
God's Word . . . and are not likely to take any part of His
revelation as seriously as they should. . . . At Mt. Sinai, God
did not show a visible symbol of Himself, but spoke to them;
therefore they are not now to seek visible images, but simply
to obey His word."[11] This does seem to be a basic problem
with many Christians.

To sum up his discussion, Packer says, "To make an image of God is to take one's own thoughts of Him from a
human source, rather than from God Himself; and this is pre-
cisely what is wrong with image-making."[12]

Widespread Visualization

In addressing Sanford's prayer of faith, I gave documentation to show that visualization is a hypnotic, occult technique based on Yoga. In health care, for example, Dr. O. Carl

Simonton, who popularized having patients visualize their cancer cells being 'gobbled up,' learned the technique from Jose Silva founder of Silva Mind Control. Bernie Siegel M.D., who channels a spirit called George, is another physician who uses visualization. He writes in his bestselling book, *Love, Medicine and Miracles,*

> The goal is to reach a light trance state, sometimes called an alpha state . . . which is the first step in hypnosis, biofeedback, yogic meditation and most related forms of mind exploration. With guidance and practice, meditation can lead to breathtaking experiences of cosmic at-oneness and enlightenment . . . among many psychological techniques . . . the most widely used and successful has been visualization or imaging.[13]

Once again, notice that visualization is not ordinary imagination. It combines hypnotic/yoga techniques with emotion, color and sound to create an altered state of consciousness.

Dual Personalities

As adults we can, and often do, behave in an immature or childish way. But to believe there actually is an inner child within us means we all have dual personalities. Or it might mean we are contacting a spirit guide which could be the inner child or a counterfeit Jesus. Johanna Michaelsen, in her book, *The Dark Side of Evil,* relates how the spirit guide she visualized as Jesus was graphically revealed later as a demon.

The inner child is not just a figure of speech. A figure of speech conveys a familiar thought but does not have a life of its own with emotions and actions. Neither is the inner child a simile: Sanford never refers to this phantom as "like an inner child." Psychologist Theodore Reik says, "In reality, there are three persons in the consultation room of the psychoanalyst: the analyst, the patient as he is now, and the child who continues his existence within the patient."[14]

Not only did Sanford regard the inner child as a living

entity, she endowed it with innocence and what seems to be original holiness; without a sin nature. This would explain why the emphasis is on comforting the child and asking forgiveness for hurting it. The inner child seems never to have done anything wrong.

I have shown Sanford's belief in the pre-existence of the soul and that the soul comes to earth trailing the wisps of heaven: "Why does beauty comfort and still my soul? Is it because this reflects the beauty and order of the heavenly kingdom from which the soul has come? . . . Our spirits evolved from the Godhead."[15] If Sanford came into this world in her original holiness, then her inner child would be of similar status. Sanford never blatantly declared the inner child is divine, but her statements bring us to this conclusion.

The impetus for the inner healing teaching that a patient needs to bring up memories which go back before birth comes from Jung's statement that the "child had a psychic life before it had consciousness."[16] This is a frequent theme in Sanford's books. She asked her readers to pray,

> And if even before birth the soul was shadowed by this human life and darkened by the fears and sorrows of the human parents, then I pray that even those memories or impressions may be healed, so that this one may be restored to Your original pattern, the soul as free and clean as though nothing had ever dimmed its shining.[17]

Secular psychology does not need to use subterfuge. Jung postulates several inner child archetypes, the most powerful being the divine inner child. James H. Young of the C. G. Jung Foundation of New York, writes, "One of the most significant features of Jung's child archetype is in its frequent function as a herald, a bringer of redemptive grace, or its ability to heal the sick and guide the lost."[18] But this psychological archetype of the inner child was developed by Freud, a militant atheist, and Jung, an agnostic who rejected Jesus as his Saviour. It predates Sanford's "Christian" inner healing movement. Obviously she and her followers took an already formulated non-Christian theology and then tried to find biblical concepts to justify this type of counseling. This is not acceptable biblical exegesis.

A review of several Jungian inner child therapists reveals a fascinating similarity between their techniques and Sanford's regimen. The only difference is the use of Jesus instead of the adult patient or some authority figure in the visualization procedure. Jungian psychologists Lucia Capacchione, John Bradshaw, Jean Houston, and Nathaniel Brandon, along with many others use essentially the same program of seeking out and "healing" the inner child.

I have chosen to quote from Nathaniel Branden. He believes when we learn to forgive this inner child, it will no longer war with the adult. To make contact with this "child self" he asks his patients to "imagine themselves walking along a country road and, in a distance to see a small child sitting by a tree and, as they draw near to see that child is the self they once were . . . [they] sit down and enter into a dialogue with the child." They are encouraged to speak aloud to deepen the reality of the experience. He has them take the child in their arms gently stroking it and letting this touch communicate acceptance and compassion; the child may or may not respond.

Brandon often has the adults look at childhood photographs then "close your eyes, take deep relaxing breaths" while they go inside themselves to explore questions put to them by him. He also uses a conditioning process where the patient finishes incomplete sentences such as, "One of the things my inner child needed when five years old was _____."[19] Of course this type of open question helps the person to bring up memories, whether they are valid memories or not.

This brings us to another objection to healing of memories of the inner child. Memories are very creative, especially when they are produced under mind-altering conditions similar to hypnosis. Courts of Law do not recognize testimony which is derived under hypnosis because of the impact of the hypnotist on the memories. Courts often also require more than one witness to validate testimony because memories of a traffic accident by those not involved can be strikingly different. My children are always correcting me on my memory of an event they also witnessed—a memory which is very vivid to me but heartily disputed by them.

For this reason we can never be certain if a memory is true, distorted or created by suggestive things said by the counselor. Memories can create havoc. Cultivating the memory only nurtures the root of bitterness. This may be why God tells us through Paul to forget those things which are behind and reach forward to the high calling of Christ Jesus (Phil. 3:13-14).

This leads us to a final yet most important indictment of the inner child. In past chapters we have discussed Sanford's distorted view of sin and forgiveness. This distorted view carries over into the idea of the inner child.

To go within oneself to the inner child, is akin to self-worship because the person is looking inward to himself rather than outward to God for comfort, healing and forgiveness. A spurious image of Jesus being present does not make it biblical. We cannot forgive ourselves. Only God can give us a new nature (2 Cor. 5:17).

I have cited Sanford and Jungian counselors to illustrate their belief that the inner child is innocent, divine, created in original holiness. If we are this divine inner child, it follows we are denying the basic Christian belief in original sin. Then, there is no need for the shed blood of Christ to reconcile us to a holy God. The inner child is a mechanism to rationalize sin. It becomes a system of works wherein we are trying to help God, or even bypass Him. We want to run our own show. But God says, "Your faith should not stand in the wisdom of men, but in the power of God; For the wisdom of this world is foolishness with God. For it is written, He taketh the wise in their own craftiness" (1 Cor. 2:5; 3:19).

The inner child system also shows a fatal lack of trust in God's wisdom and omniscience and His ability "to bring it to pass" (Prov. 3:5-6). If we have been washed in the blood of the Lamb and repent of our daily sins then we can rest in His finished work. Hebrews 4:9-10 tells us, "There remaineth therefore a rest unto the people of God. For he that entereth into his rest, he also hath ceased from his own works, as God did from his." What a struggle to go, time after time, into an altered state of consciousness to contact our inner child and a spirit guide; this is not resting in the promises of God. It reminds me of the priests in the Old Testament who daily, year after year, sacrificed animals. When Jesus came he offered Himself once and for all and the old covenant priestly system ended (Heb 7:27).

Do we believe God or do we not? Dare we call Him a liar by devising our own system to handle our sins or the sins of others against us? Is there no God in America that we have to consult an inner child and a phantom Jesus as Israel cosulted Baal-Zebub (2 Kings 1:3, 16)? As Christians we must be careful to not go a-whoring after the other gods of Jungian depth psychology.

Chapter Fifteen:

The Source of the Unconscious

Non-Christian thought won a great victory when much of American Christianity embraced the Freudian concept of the unconscious. It is part of everyday vocabulary; it is used to excuse even sinful actions. Agnes Sanford's theology of healing draws heavily on the Freudian and Jungian notions of the unconscious.

Social scientist Lancelot Whyte in his book, *The Unconscious Before Freud*, calls the "idea of the unconscious the supreme revolutionary conception of the modern age: it undermines the traditional foundations of Europe and the West."[1] Since the traditional foundation of the West is the Judeo-Christian ethic, Whyte's statement really means the idea of the unconscious undermines Christian thought.

In terms of a Christian framework, we agree that we are conscious of those items within our attention, and at the same time, we are not directly conscious of many of our bodily and mental processes. This is the way God created us. He created our autonomic nervous system (sympathetic and parasympathetic) which regulates our heart, digestive system, and other organs to maintain the stability of our internal bodily environment. All of this is done without our conscious control. In like manner, our brain automatically processes much of our thinking. If we consciously managed all the variables which enter into the formulation of our speech and thought, we would have time for a only few thoughts each day. The mechanism behind thought and speech could be likened to the complicated processes of a computer of which we are unaware each time we punch the keys.

Many people would point to Freud as the source of the theory of the unconscious. Some writers associate its origin with Mesmer and Mesmerism and have pointed out its relationship with hypnotism.

Man has always speculated about how the brain functions and how thoughts form, how the words can come flowing forth when we speak and write. These reflections have lead to spiritism in "pagan" cultures and philosophy in "sophisticated" society. Philosophy predated dynamic psychiatry. Such agnostic philosophers as Goethe, Schopenhauer, and Nietzsche influenced Freud and Jung. Whyte says Nietzsche's passionate temperament "sought to replace Christianity by a doctrine of vital energy as the source of everything natural, human and divine. He never doubted that the conscious mind is the instrument of unconscious vitality."[2]

But the major root of dynamic psychiatry and its theory of the unconscious are found elsewhere. Psychiatrist Henri F. Ellenberger has written one of the most comprehensive histories of dynamic psychiatry which culminated in the psychiatric systems of Janet, Freud, Adler and Jung.

> This survey has historical interest because a continuous chain can be demonstrated between exorcism and magnetism, magnetism and hypnotism, hypnotism and the great modern dynamic systems. . . . The advent of spiritism in the years 1848 to 1853 meant a decisive turning point in the history of dynamic psychiatry.[3]

In another chapter he states, "The advent of spiritism was an event of major importance in the history of dynamic psychiatry because it indirectly provided new approaches to the mind."[4]

Mediums and Mesmerists

We also find through Ellenberger that "the beginning of dynamic psychiatry featured the use of mediums as an approach to the unconscious mind."[5] The ancestry of psychiatry is therefore very pertinent to the theory of the unconscious and whether Christians should incorporate it in their counseling. Ellenberger traces the roots of psychiatric techniques back in time to primitive peoples. He cites historical and anthropological research which established the use of many of the methods of modern psychotherapy by their shamans (witch doctors) and medicine men. He takes up at length the role of exorcism in the evolution of psychotherapy. Practitioners believed that all problems were due to evil spirits possessing the person. The spirits could be exorcised by conjurations and other psychic means.[6]

A fascinating section of Ellengers's book shows the transition from exorcism to Mesmerism. Many equate Mesmerism with hypnosis, but Mesmer's unique explanation for his healing skills differ from modern hypnotism. In 1779, Mesmer explained his system of animal magnetism with 27 points, teaching that an unknown fluid fills the universe connecting the stars and planets to man. Health or disease depends on the balance of this fluid in the body. If one used the proper technique, the fluid could be channeled to another person and a "crisis" provoked which cured the disease or hysteria.

The transition to artificial somnambulism (artificial sleep-walking) which Dr. James Braid of England later called hypnotism occurred when a French nobleman, Marquis de Puysegur, embraced the practice of Mesmerism. He treated a young peasant, Victor Race, who manifested an unusual crisis. Instead of convulsions or other disorderly movements, Race entered a strange sleep-state in which he was more awake or aware than when normally conscious. He also had no memory of the event when the crisis (sleep state) passed. Puysegur soon was deluged with patients. He also researched artificial somnambulism and concluded that a psychosis might be a somnambulic crisis. He suggested the use of hypnotism in hospitals to cure the insane.

Abbe Faria, a Portuguese priest who claimed to be born a Hindu Brahmin, taught lucid sleep in Paris beginning in 1813. He introduced sitting patients in comfortable chairs. He had them fixate on his hand. Then he commanded loudly, "Sleep!" While in magnetic sleep, they saw visions and conformed to posthypnotic suggestion. Others recognized that hypnosis involved autosuggestion—the ability to hypnotize oneself. They also noticed mutual suggestion, such as persons who were more receptive to hypnosis if they saw others hypnotized.

Jean Martin Charcot, very famous in medical history, considered hypnosis to be a pathological condition confined to hysterics. But Hippolyte Bertheim, who headed the Nancy (France) school of hypnotists contended hypnosis was all due to suggestion and the effects obtained could be equally obtained by suggestion in the waking state, a procedure the Nancy School termed "psychotherapeutics." Bertheim also emphasized that pseudo-memories can be suggested. Healing of memories counselors employ similar tactics, using suggestion and leading questions to help the patient bring up what may be pseudo-memories.

The early mesmerists and hypnotists recognized dangers and drawbacks to their therapy which still apply today. "It became evident that a hypnotized subject is perfectly able to lie, not only through suggestion, but of his own volition."[7] They recognized the dangers of addiction to hypnosis and abnormal dependence on the therapist, precipitating a psychosis, and vigilambulism, which is a permanent half-somnambulism where the subject seems to be fully awake but is liable to suggestion from persons other than the hypnotist.

Until the middle of the nineteenth century hypnosis was the basic "window" into the unconscious. Then spiritism became dominant when mediums began to write as spirits dictated to them. Janet, a contemporary of Freud, routinely used automatic writing to investigate the subconscious. Jung related an episode which occurred when he was writing under the "dictation of the unconscious." He asked himself, "Is this really science what I am doing?" A woman's voice answered him and they conversed for awhile. From this he deduced he had within himself an autonomous feminine subpersonality he named his 'anima.'[8]

Jung and Spiritualism

The advent of spiritism had brought forth a new type of individual: the medium. Much is common to both hypnotic sleep and the self-induced trance of the medium but material produced by the latter is more spontaneous and likely to be more original. It was a great step forward for dynamic psychiatry when Flournoy at the end of the nineteenth century, followed soon by C. G. Jung, undertook a systematic investigation of mediums.

We find further evidence of Jung's use of mediums. He gave a course on the History of Psychology in 1933-34 at the Swiss Polytechnical School of Zurich. "The greater part of the course was devoted to Justinus Kerner and the Seeress of Prevost. Flournoy was also given recognition for his five-year study of Catherine Muller who used the pseudonym of Helen Smith."[9] Catherine was a medium. In 1898 Jung was involved in spiritistic experiments with his cousin, Helene Preiswerk, a medium who channelled a spirit called Ivenes. "This was an important episode in Jung's life."[10]

We touched on Jung's involvement with Preiswerk earlier. He used the notes gathered from experiments on this young medium in his dissertation for his medical degree. "Here we find several of Jung's most basic ideas in their embryonic state."[11] Jung spoke to the Basel Zofingia (students association) in defense of spiritism which to him was not occult but unknown psychic phenomena which should be studied scientifically. Jung also conducted experiments years later in the 1920s with a famous Austrian medium, Rudi Schneider. His interest in mediums continued at least through the 1930s.

Jung also had a spirit guide called Philemon. He encountered Philemon during his creative illness or "confrontation with the unconscious." The symptoms of a creative illness begin after a period of restless intellectual work and involve depression, exhaustion, sleeplessness, irritability and headaches. The person is obsessed by a prevailing idea, lives in spiritual isolation and has the feeling no one can help him. The illness lasts three or more years but recovery is spontaneous and rapid and marked by euphoria. The patient is convinced that he has gained access to a new spiritual truth or world. Ellingberger cites Freud, Jung, Nietzsche and certain mystics, shamans, and philosophers as conceiving their original ideas during the agony of a creative illness.

Jung wrote of a period between 1913 and 1919 when he undertook a journey through his unconscious. He called it his Nekyia after an episode in Homer's Odyssey: the "Journey of Ulysses to the Sojourn of the Dead." Jung, by forced imagination and drawing pictures of his dreams, directed his fantasies to imagine he was digging into underground caves where he encountered many weird figures, among them his wise spirit guide Philemon. From Philemon, Jung learned "man can teach himself things of which he is not aware."[12]

Besides Philemon, on Jung's fantasized journey into the earth, he met Elias, a blind woman, Salome and his anima. Michael Harner, professor of anthropology and himself a shaman, relates in his book, *The Way of the Shaman*, how he and Native American witch doctors go into the earth while in an altered state of consciousness, in order to find power for their lives from spirit guides (power animals).[13] "Jung says he was able to achieve this descent into Hades and emerge victoriously from a perilous experiment."[14] Jung also claimed Nietzsche had a similar experience but was overwhelmed. Nietzsche lapsed into permanent insanity while Jung's creative illness lasted only a few years.

Jung's outward behavior also spoke of a psychosis. Jung had been an unabashed admirer and champion of Freud. He became Freud's "Crown Prince," president of the International Psychoanalytic Association and editor for its journal, Jahrbuch. The relationship between Jung and Freud gradually soured and turned bitter. In 1913, Jung officially broke with Freud by resigning as president of the analytic association. This crisis overwhelmed him. He severed most of his professional and social activities. He resigned as professor at Zurich University. He spent long periods of time brooding by the lake or hours piling stones one on top of the other. "Jung survived the onslaught of the unconscious alone. . . . It should be noted that this kind of inner journey is a dangerous process. . . ."[15]

During Jung's journey through the unconscious, he solidified his theories about archetypes which led to his unique teaching about a collective unconscious. Jung served as a psychiatrist at the Burgholzli hospital for the insane in Zurich for nine years. He was impressed with the marked similarity of symbols in the delusions and hallucinations of Schizophrenics to symbols in myths and the psychic life of primitive tribes. These universal symbols he called archetypes. He postulated that these symbols, common to the myths of primitive cultures and to contemporary psychotics, must be an unconscious part of the mental life of normal persons.

Jung related how the idea of archetypes first came to him. A psychotic man who hallucinated almost continually claimed he saw the sun with a phallus whose movements produced the wind. Jung was unable to explain this delusion until he read Dietrich's book on religious history. This book, written about a just published Greek papyrus on the Mithraic religion, mentioned the wind originating in a tube hanging from the sun. So Jung felt the only explanation for this delusion was universal symbols found in religious myths, fantasy, and psychotic delusions.

If symbols are common to the unconscious, it follows in Jungian thought that there must be a collective unconscious common to all men. The inner healing Agnes Sanford and her disciples offer the Christian stands on this doctrine of the universal or collective unconscious.

The structure of Freudian and Jungian psychoanalysis is significant. Soon after Freud developed his theories, he estab-

lished his own organization and publishing house. Psychoanalysis had its strict rules of membership and official doctrine. Above all, Freud demanded total control over what
was to be considered as psychoanalysis and what was not.

> Both [Freud and Jung] underwent a creative illness in a spon-
> taneous and original form, and both made them a model to
> be followed by their disciples under the name of training
> analysis. Jung promoted the training analysis, and the Freud-
> ians accepted it for its didactic value but the Jungian school
> later came to accept it as a kind of initiatory malady compa-
> rable to the shaman.[16]

By their very definitions the unconscious and subconscious
are outside or below our normal state of consciousness. There
fore they are unknown. Freud himself said, "We call 'unconscious' any mental process the existence of which we obliged
to *assume*." British psychologist J. A. C. Brown, author of a
textbook on psychology, said, "Jung's theory of archtypes is
a further example of his peculiar attitude to the scientific
method, and in this instance we find him describing the par-
tially known in terms of the totally unknown."[17]

   Why should we believe there is an unconscious when the
so-called evidence comes from abnormal minds and from
mediums channeling spirits? Why should Christians become
involved in this sort of thinking? Why should we believe in
the unconscious when there is not a shred of evidence for it
in the Bible?

   "Beware lest any man spoil you through philosophy and
vain deceit, after the tradition of men, after the rudiments of
this world, and not after Christ" (Col. 2:8).

Chapter Sixteen:

The Collective Unconscious

Caught by birth and marriage in orthodox Christianity, Sanford could not openly rebel. Instead, she took the path of syncretism wherein she attempted to unite Christianity with New Thought and Jungian depth therapy.

She had always been bothered by the shedding of blood. This led her to the theory that Jesus' blood dripped onto the earth, mixed with the dust, was blown into the air, and remains in the air we breathe today as an invisible current of heavenly energy. This theory in turn led to believing that Christ's blood was not to justify us but to be used as a power we breath into our bodies to help our sanctification.

The Cross was her big stumbling block. From Fox's book, *The Sermon on the Mount*, she glimpsed the answer which solved her dilemma—"thought vibrations" and Jung's theory of the unconscious and collective unconscious. New Thought had embraced the unconscious with enthusiasm for it enlarged the dynamic of the "Divine Mind.' They often couched it in somewhat different terms. For example, Ernest Holmes, the founder of Science of Mind, calls the subconscious the subjective mind, and the collective unconscious the race-suggestion, or One Subjective Mind.[1]

The Work of the Cross

How did Agnes Sanford get around the Cross? She explained in her first book,

> He [Jesus] tried saving people by his teaching alone and it did not work. . . . They were short-circuited . . . by the negative thought-vibrations of this sinful world. . . . So our Lord in the Garden of Gethsemane undertook the great work we call the atonement—the at-one-ment. . . . He literally lowered His thought vibrations to the thought vibrations of humanity and received unto Himself man's thoughts of sin and sickness, pain and death.[2]

In her subsequent books she abandoned thought vibrations and used collective unconscious to express essentially the same idea.

> How did He take into Himself our griefs and our sorrows, beginning His passion in the Garden of Gethsemane. . . . There is a pathway between spirit and heart or subconscious. But this pathway was twisted and warped by long denial of God's words. . . . It was choked by sand and silt. . . . But in order to redeem the human race it was necessary to sink deeper into humanity: to become part of the subconscious mind of every man. Jesus Christ opened the channel between the subconscious and the spirit . . . taking the dirt from the mass subconscious of the race into Himself, then throwing it away upon the shore of God's Being.[3]

> He became a man potentially when he was born of the Virgin Mary. But when He entered upon His great work of redemption in the Garden. . . . He became Man, Mankind. . . . He became a very part of the collective unconsciousness of the race. . . . He became forever a part of the mass mind of the race.[4]

Here she combined two theories. First, she believed in "redemptive suffering." She believed Jesus suffered because "all the griefs and sorrows of mankind rolled in upon Him"[5] in the Garden of Gethsemane, as well as on the Cross. This suffering, not His shed blood, brought about our reconciliation with God. She spent an entire chapter in *The Healing Touch of God* explaining this.

Second, she said Jesus actually entered into the dirt (sin) of the collective conscious. If this were true Jesus would have become a sinner like us and would not have been the spotless "Lamb of God which taketh away the sin of the world" (John 1:29). He would just be another man separated from God. If Jesus entered into the dirt of the mass mind and still went to His Father, then we would have that capability ourselves. We could save ourselves. All of this negates the blood of Jesus which was shed for us that we might be justified and reconciled to the holy God.

Collective Conscious

Sanford also used the collective unconscious in her concept of healing and her peculiar ideas about sanctification.

> He can enter below the level of consciousness. He can project His life back through time in me and heal my oldest and most hidden memories, so that as His power works in the submerged mind, my outer reactions and my conscious thoughts more and more conform to the image of His joy and light.[6]

Here she affirmed the Freudian doctrine used in all psychological therapy that the unconscious is a powerful dark force which rules our conscious lives.

> For He saw our need, and knew that while our conscious mind could learn and keep the laws of God, the subconscious mind bound and hampered by unhappy memories, needed help in order to do so. If the girl . . . could have seen and grasped His power of transcending time for her she could have been set free from those troubling memories and thought-habits and could have been made a new creature.[7]

2 Corinthians 5:17 is the only verse which speaks about becoming a new creature: "Therefore if any man be in Christ,
he is a new creature, old things are passed away; behold all
things are become new." This passage does not mention
time-traveling with Jesus to be set free of painful memories;
it speaks of abiding in Christ. And of course, to abide we
must first be reconciled to God.

In Sanford's account of this girl above, there is no indi-
cation the woman had a personal relationship with Jesus nor
did Sanford speak to her of this. Sanford did tell her to pray
for a "sense of guilt." "Thus I tried to help her but failed.
She did not want to keep the laws of God. She wanted to
continue to break them." Naturally she would, for "The natural
man receiveth not the things of the Spirit of God: for they
are foolishness unto him; neither can he know them, because
they are spiritually discerned." (1 Cor. 2:13).

Sanford wrote frequently about becoming the sons of
God, combining Romans 8:19 and John 1:12. Sometimes she
wrote about salvation and other times about sanctification.
The following remark pertained to salvation:

> His love would reach not only the conscious but also the
> subconscious mind of man and redeem the imagination of
> man's heart. Thus mankind would become the first fruits
> of a new order of being, namely, the sons of God.[8]

Sanford also wrote about the real possibility Christians
had of becoming Sons of God who would not see death
but would remain to heal the earth and thus bring about the
Kingdom of God. She believed that God had planned this
before the creation of Adam and Eve.

> Apparently God had in mind a plan for man's evolving step
> by step into a being not subject to death . . . in hopes that
> among this race there may evolve the sons of God.[9]

What then is the ultimate work that God's Holy Spirit can
do within us? What is the highest of which this mortal

body is capable? Can the day come when God's Spirit can so quicken this body that it shall be spiritualized and resurrected in every cell and become white upon this earth, a body like unto the body of Jesus Christ? . . . But whether any of us in this present life can attain to this final will of God . . . that is another question. It depends on us personally. . . also the amount of spiritual power available in the whole Church.[10]

Then this concept evolved into what I call 'spiritual ecology.' Using John 3:16, she wrote that the

Bible says it was because God so loved the world—the work of His hands or of His Holy imagination—that He sent His Son to die for the sins of the little people on one planet, the earth, so that these people might become the sons of God and take care of the earth that He put in their charge."[11]

"For He came down to earth, and died on the Cross not to destroy us but to save us, not to wreck the little planet earth but to transform it into the Kingdom of heaven."[12] Jesus gave us the mandate to bring in the kingdom of God ("heal the earth") in the Lord's Prayer because "The earth can feel God's love and respond to prayer."[13]

Rationale for her spiritual ecology depended in part on her view of redemption—Jesus died to redeem planet earth.

Man was tempted to do wrong that good might come, to bring about a reform or a growth of his soul by breaking God's commandments.[14]

The invisible energy of the earth was changed by the violence of man. And from the earth and by the earth Cain was punished. Adam and Eve mourned continually for the garden--but not all their tears and cries could restore their heritage. [For] Jesus Christ had not yet come to the earth to mingle his blood with the blood of Abel who was slain, and to redeem the earth.[15]

Sanford tried to help heal the earth by praying for "the healing of the earth itself. I tried this first in praying for hurricanes to quiet down."[16] The result was, "My friends and I could pray away a hurricane in an almost laughable manner if it were coming toward the east coast."[17] She moved to California after Ted died and prayed "continually for the healing of the San Andreas fault. . . . I pray for the peace of God to enter into the San Andreas fault itself. I even pray for the 'fire angels'. . . to enter in and accomplish a work of healing."[18] She admitted she did not know what the 'fire angels' were.

She became quite imperious in commanding the elements:

> I advised the jet stream to move over in the name of the Lord in whatever was the best way to cause rain in that part of the country. Then I spoke to the wind and said, 'Now swing around and blow from the far sea, bring a gentle rain to the thirsty fields.' That night the rain began.[19]

Certainly her mentor, Emmet Fox, influenced her when he wrote,

> The spiritual key is the undeniable fact that the whole of the outer world—whether it be the physical body, the common things of life, the winds and the rain, the clouds and the earth itself—is amenable to man's thought and he has dominion over it when he knows it.[20]

Necessity of Earth Healing

Although she made an erroneous interpretation of the Lord's Prayer, the real foundation for healing the earth is Sanford's unbiblical, almost pagan belief in the nature of God. As noted earlier, she believed God is in and a part of nature—an energy similar to light which flowed in and through herself and every created thing. The earth therefore is an actual sentient being needing to be healed before Jesus returns. She devoted her book, *Creation Waits*, entirely to this theme.

We have examined the foundation and the mandate for

healing of the earth. Now let us look at why the earth has need for healing. Sanford had a fascinating explanation. She related it to the story of Cain and Abel.

> Cain in his dissatisfaction with himself hated his brother. . . . The hatred of his heart reflected itself upon the earth which sought a means of revenging itself on him. So the earth itself rejected him. . . . We read in this old story that the invisible energy of the earth was changed by the violence of man and from the earth and by the earth Cain was punished. The earth no longer brought forth its increase for his use. . . . Cain could not take away the stain of his brother's blood from the ground, but in Jesus, God Himself came to take away the poison of contamination from the earth. (Rom 8:1) The power of His sacrifice is now released to the earth and it is for us to apply it.[21]

How? She said we apply this power by using creative imagination which entails making "in our minds the picture of a world at peace . . . as the kingdom of God. . . . For every thought-form of evil we send forth . . . tends to create evil, or to fasten upon the world the present evil."[22]

I think we can say with confidence Sanford used the unconscious in structuring her view of redemption and sanctification which also led to these other unusual beliefs about the earth and the sons of God. Did Sanford use the Freudian and Jungian unconscious and collective unconscious to structure her thoughts on faith healing and inner healing also? Most certainly.

What is Memory Really All About?

When Freud postulated his theories that "repressed" memories form infancy and childhood were the roots of emotional trauma, the anatomy of the brain was known, but how it functioned was not known. Thus a person could postulate anything they wanted to about memory. Now however, there has been an explosion of knowledge about memory in the last ten years which shoots down the wild postulates of Healing of Memories counselors.

Some of the pertinent findings can be summarized as I have them below.

1. In any kind of strong emotional experience, the brain utilizes the "fight or flight" reaction of the body with its out-pouring of adrenalin and noradenaline to regulate the strength of the storage of memory so that the memory becomes virtually indelible. This is the conclusion of research done by Roger Pittman, M.D, of Harvard. Dr. Paul McHugh of Johns Hopkins University Hospital concurs that people just don't forget important traumae that happen to them but in fact they are remembered all too well; they can't be forgotten.

2. Twenty-five percent of individuals can easily be induced to remember events that never happened to them, false memories that feel absolutely real. Elizabeth Loftus, University of Washington psychologist and expert on memory and suggestibility, says there is virtually no scientific documentation that memories can be repressed and reliably recovered. She is able to prompt volunteers to "remember" non-existent broken glass and tape recorders; to think of a clean shaven man as having a mustache; of straight hair as curly; to place a barn in a bucolic scene that contained no building; to believe in events that never happened.

3. Many researchers have concluded that a repressed memory which emerges decades later is probably rare and my be due to invention. Most experts agree that human memory is not like a video cassette player, faithfully replaying the sme scenes; that memory is malleable and so are we.

4. The American Medical Association in 1993 passed a resolution condemning the "misuse of hypnosis and other techniques in memory enhancement." A False memory Syndrome Foundation was established in 1992 and within a year

they claimed 7,000 families as members. A suit has been successfully prosecuted when a jury in Napa, California, found two therapists conjured up false memories in a patient. Six major books on the fallibility of memory were published last year.

5. Declarative memory develops late, two to three years into life. Emory University cognitive psychologist Ulric Neisser's research indicates people can't recall what happened before the age of two unless it was a repetitive act such as drinking from a bottle. Before the age of one, they can't remember anything because the hippocampus where the brain processes episodic memories does not mature until then. Neisser notes that necessary psychological structures have not matured then, either.

Besides calling into question the validity of childhood "repressed" memories, research has destroyed absolutely the idea of recalling memories which go back to the womb or time of conception. Apparently God created us with the inability to recall the events of our gestation and birth.

Those who claim to be Christians and use Healing of Memories in their counseling stand on a shaky foundation which is not of God.

Dreaming

One aspect of healing we have not yet addressed also involves the unconscious—dreams. Sanford's son John, an Episcopalian priest who studied at the Jung Institute in Switzerland, taught her about dream interpretation. Distilled into elemental terms, dream therapists postulate that dreams are an expression of the unconscious activity which governs our conscious life. These dreams, thoughts of the unconscious, are expressed in symbols, images and myths (archetypes) which must be interpreted.

Sanford expressed Jung's ideas in her writing:

When man could no longer hear the direct speech of God, then the Creator spoke to him through the dark speech of dreams, moving mysteriously in the deep unconscious and often using symbols that the conscious mind does not comprehend til its understanding is opened. These symbols and dream images are frequently of great antiquity, coming out of the collective unconscious of the race.[23]

Sanford buttressed her belief in dreams by writing about modern research into sleep which has shown there are different stages of sleep. Dreaming is accompanied by certain rapid eye movements, thus the name REM sleep. Since the time she tried to justify dreams as a product of the unconscious, further scientific research has negated this concept which Freud and Jung taught as fact. Freud, in his paper "The Project for a Scientific Psychology," tried and failed to give it a scientific basis.

Michel Jouvet, a French neuro-physiologist, discovered in the 1960s that while the muscles are relaxed in sleep, the brain stem inhibits the nerves carrying input from the external world and sends PGO waves (pulses of excitation) to the brain cortex which remains very active.

J. Allan Hobson and Robert W. McCarley of Harvard Medical School say this explains why a dream does not begin with an unconscious wish rising from the unconscious.[24] Dreams contain vivid hallucinations, distortions of time, place and person, and emotionally charged subjects for physiological not psychological reasons. No visual or motor messages from the outside stimulate the cortex of the brain; the cerebral cortex is excited by messages sent by the brain stem and the cortex processes them as if they were coming from external stimuli. Distortions are caused by the distorted nature of the PGO waves from the brain stem.

Hobson says a dream is "the awareness of an auto-activated mind." A dream does not begin with an unconscious symbol or archetype coming out of the unconscious but is the effort of the higher center of the brain trying to unscramble the meaningless signals sent from the lower brain stem. Out of nonsense the brain tries to create sense.

While Sanford believed in dreams in the Freudian-Jungian sense, she did not utilize them in therapy as her son John or her Pastor Morton Kelsey do. Both have written books on dream analysis. Instead of analysis, Sanford sought to experience visions in her own life. I have commented previously about her visions of being caught up into "heaven" and the "New Jerusalem," her vision of Jesus giving her 'sealed orders' before her birth to bring a new gospel of healing to earth.

I am saddened to realize this talented, charming woman was so deceived by New Thought and Jungian psychology. She can't plead ignorance of the Bible because she acknowledged that she memorized Scripture and read through the Bible each year with her missionary parents. I am saddened even more because many Christians have been deceived through her books, lectures and Schools of Pastoral Care.

Chapter Seventeen:

Agnes's Legacy:
The Ministry of John Sandford

John Sandford is the most influential disciple of Agnes Sanford. John and Paula Sandford acknowledge their debt to Agnes Sanford in their books, and John relates many anecdotes about his ministry with Agnes. "Of course no list of acknowledgments could be complete in a book concerning the healing of the inner man which does not give thanks for the pioneering work of Agnes Sanford. She was also our own mentor in the Lord, our friend and advisor. It was her common sense which first hauled our soaring mysticism to safe moorings in sound theology, the Word of God and earthiness." [1]

John Sandford's Autobiographical Data:
- "Our family has always been mystical." [2]
- "I was the super-spook mystic always having dreams, seeing visions, and having far-out experiences." [3]
- "In earlier years I lost track of reality for a few hours several times." [4]
- "I became interested in Rosicrucianism, read some mediumistic books." [5]
- "Along the way a demon had entered." [6]
- "Surely that demonic thing must have warped my theology and my sermons." [7]
- The demon was exorcised in 1958. [8]

Pantheism:

- "God is in all and through all, touching us. I have wept in spirit as I watched my dead-in-spirit friends crush a lily without a thought or spark of awareness."[9]
- "The elusive energy behind the electron is the very Spirit of God."[10]
- "Matter is some form of expression of Spirit."[11]
- "God breathed His own holy breath into him (man)."[12] [Genesis 2:7 says breath of life]
- "The Holy Spirit inhabits all of our spirit, like pouring red dye into blue resulting in purple."[13]
- "God's Spirit flows according to His principles . . . through all that is, like electricity within its laws."[14]
- "It is crucial to our understanding of prayer to comprehend that this Spirit or energy flows in and through *all* things."[15]

Pre-existence

- "We do not know whether our spirit came to earth from Heaven, having some sort of pre-existence there, or it begins with conception. . . . I do tend most of the time to think we must have been with the Father and that our Lord asked us to come, but no one knows for sure."[16]
- "However, our Spirit knew the beauty and wholesomeness of Heaven. Our Spirit remembers what it was like to be at one with the Creator, whether through millenia of heavenly dwelling or in a moment of creation. . . . Imagine then the effect upon a pure and pristine spirit upon becoming part of this earth's corruption."[17]

Gethsemane:

- "By becoming as us in Gethsemane, our Lord Jesus Christ gained the right (necessitated by our free will) to die for us on the cross."[18]
- "When Jesus left heaven to come to earth He became a

man. But yet He remained one individual by himself. In the Garden He became mankind [the collective unconscious]. Until the agony He endured in the garden, His death on the cross might possibly have meant little, for He would only have died alone, as himself only affecting little, other than by example."[19]

• "The law of Christ is intercession. If we are daily willing to become loaded with the rottenness of others [burden bearing], to 'watch' with Jesus in Gethsemane, then the death of the cross will be at work in us for others, that His life may be at work in others. Thus we save Our lives by being where that life is. Jesus is that life, and He goes continually to Gethsemane for others through us."[20]

• In Gethsemane "He accomplished the work of empathetic identification or burden bearing which made the cross effective.... Gethsemane was integrally necessary to the accomplishment of redemption by His death on the cross."[21]

Psychology:

• "Whatever we say is psychologically sound. We treasure the insights of psychology."[22]

• John's use of Carl Jung's terms: tower, father of the man, heart = the unconscious, amniosis, archetypes, anima and anumus—the same as Jung, except that they are expressed as male and female in all of us—individuation, collective unconscious, rebirthing, fragmentation or lack of integration adepts, latent language.[23] John, "to borrow a term from Carl Jung," defines "An archetype as a ruling way of thinking, feeling, and acting . . . not inside an individual but in the flesh of mankind [collective unconscious] . . . which acts upon us to control us individually . . . we become robots programmed to perform, manipulated by forces outside ourselves."[24]

The Counselor:

• "First, he is a father-confessor. . . . Hearing the confession of another . . . pronounces forgiveness as a part of his priesthood in the priesthood of all believers."[25]

• "Pronounce forgiveness in the first person. . . . I pronounce you are forgiven. . . . It is not as effective merely to say, 'Your sins are forgiven in Jesus' name' or 'The Bible says you are forgiven.' When a man sins, that sin denigrates mankind . . . mankind has been injured; mankind needs to forgive. Our saying 'I forgive you' is essential to accomplish forgiveness, from man."[26]

• "How do we minister to the lost and abused and wounded lambs in the name of Jesus? By repentence on behalf of those who are abusers . . . we find it effective to express our repentance verbally in the presence of the wounded one. If *the* parents of an abused child have been unable to ask forgiveness, it is of some comfort for the child to hear those words expressed sincerely by *a* parent."[27]

• "The intercessor is to make himself a channel for the grace of repentance by acting out that repentence before it comes to one for whom he prays."[28]

• "Immediately as we went through banal chitchat, I began to intercede and repent silently for the man."[29]

• "By pronouncing absolution (assurance of forgiveness)."[30]

• "If he hears a confession of sexual immorality he should pronounce absolution, seek out and forgive roots, transform . . . I loose you in Jesus name, grateful that what I loose on earth *is* loosed in heaven."[31]

Admiration for Roman Catholicism:

The preceding quotations demonstrate the Sandfords' Roman Catholic slant to their counseling. At their Elijah House, "two Roman Catholic members" counsel.[32]

• "We often attend a nearby, Friday night Catholic charismatic meeting."[33]

• "I still love a Catholic charismatic Mass far above all other forms of worship."[34]

- "As God pours out His Spirit on all flesh, we see the Catholic Communion [mass] 'turning again' and becoming a source of strength to its brethren in all communions of Christendom."[35]
- "For God intends to turn the age of division into the age of unity, causing each arm of His body to present what it has sculpted from the rock of truth as a gift to the whole church," for example "what God has sustained and prospered among Catholics as the mass, concepts of authority, and liturgical devotion."[36]

New Age:
- "Faith embraces a trichotomy of mind, heart or unconscious, and spirit."[37]
- "There may be [with inner vows] a heart of stone or unconscious."[38]
- "Faith adds that our spirits can intuitively grasp knowledge far beyond the mind even without God's help."[39]
- "Turned on and tuned in people have dreams or visions or hear the Lord speak directly . . . have intuitive hunches."[40]
- "The final degree of vision occurs by trance."[41]

The Occult:
- "Some informative dreams I call 'medicine' dreams . . . borrowed from my Osage Indian heritage. Each brave, coming to maturity fasted and prayed that Wahkontah, the great spirit, Would give him signs or dreams to indicate his purpose in life. . . . Thus we use the term to describe a dream that significantly affects our purpose in the Kingdom of God."[42]
- Sandford relates he was in "spiritual warfare with a coven of witches" when he was told "there's something evil" in his back. A "woman who possessed a keen gift of discernment . . . prayed in the Spirit and then grabbed forcefully exactly on that spot in my back, and jerked something out

and away from me, screaming in fear of it . . . it was a spear, an evil thing of Satan."[43] Michael Harner, an anthropologist and shaman, describes in his book shamans extracting harmful power intrusions from the body.[44]

• "When I identified spiritually with Jo, nobody was home . . . recalling J.R.R. *Tolkien's Lord of the Rings* gave me an idea. . . . I sent my spirit with the Lord's to find Jo. He did it by a vision."[45] The lengthy vision Sandford describes is like a journey down into the earth as recounted by Jung and native American shamans.[46]

• Sandford writes, "Symbols are the peculiar language of dreams. To better understand symbols a study of comparative religion, or some anthology of myths will help."[47]

Aura, Extra Sensory Perception:

• Noting there are invisible radio and TV waves, Sanford says, "Our spirits have 'vibes' or energies or some kind of rays which reach beyond our bodies."[48]

• "The third basic function of our spirit is to reach out across space beyond the body and sometimes beyond the five senses to meet and interact with others."[49]

• "Many life-after-death books universally speak of the spirit leaving and returning to the body."[50]

Generational Sin:

• "The fifth function of our personal spirit is to enable us to transcend time."[51]

• "First, we spend considerable time asking the counselee to relate (what) he can recall of the family history. We call for the blood of Jesus to flow back through the family blood lines throughout their history, by forgiveness washing away . . . Satan's attack."[52]

• "In this prayer, we are not merely praying for the counselee, but for him in proxy for his entire family . . . living or has already died. . . . About half of the church believes it is forbidden to pray for the departed, and half [Catholics] are commanded to pray for the deceased. There need be no quarrel. Let each brother pray 'according to the proportion of his faith.'"[53]

Inner Healing:

• "All of us, having formed hearts of stone [a heart of stone or unconscious] have to that degree failed to become fully human."[54]

• "It is Jesus who became flesh to meet and melt hearts of stone to give us hearts of flesh."[55]

• "It is Jesus who makes us human."[56]

• "Our *spirits* are washed clean at the moment of conversion (though they may need it again and again). But not all the heart has yet agreed or received."[57]

• "Their inner spirit is angry and hurt, whether the mind and heart are aware of it or not."[58]

Healing Of Memories:

In the Sandfords' books and counseling ministries, healing of memories is the foundation to all their therapies for healing "bitter root judgement and expectancy," "inner vows," "hearts of stone," "the slumbering spirit," "spiritual imprisonment," "generational sin," and others.[59]

• "The Lord revealed that He had brought Barbara and me together that we as a Catholic laywomen and a Protestant minister might pray for the healing of memories and reconciliation of the Catholic and Protestant churches . . . through the entire history from 1515 to the present . . . applying the blood and cross of Christ . . . prayed for the healing [of memories] of every occasion in which Catholics and Protestants had married, and then been cast out of one or both churches."[60]

• The Sandfords emphasize healing of memories goes as far back as "in utero experiences" even though "insights con-

cerning our personal spirit from the time of conception seem
not so clearly laid out in the word of God as were our earlier
teachings."[61]

• "The reality of Jesus affecting the spirit of a person is
made possible through prayer for the innermost being of the
tiny child inside the one for whom you pray. Jesus Christ is
not confined to the dimensions of time and place. . . . He can
identify with and heal a wounded spirit all the way back to
the time of conception."[62]

• The Sandfords use suggestion: We "routinely ask questions concerning early childhood. . . . You say your husband
never listens to you? Tell me about your father. Did he give
you affection? *etc.* Usually we ask several general questions
first and then slip in relevant ones so as to camouflage our
intent."[63]

• "I explained that the spirit of a young child experiences
far more than he can know with his mind. . . . I told him. . . .
The young man consented to offer to God, on faith, what he
could imagine might have been."[64]

The Inner Child:

• "We are incarnate beings [not created?]. That means
we are not spirits *in* a body, as water fills a can. We are spiritual bodies. . . . Our spirit *becomes* flesh."[65]

• "Life-after-death books speak of the spirit leaving and
returning to the body."[66]

• "The fifth function of our personal spirit is to enable
us to transcend time."[67]

• "We have stated that Jesus is able to transcend time and
identify with us at *any* stage of our development to set us free
from those dated emotions and expectations . . . which hold
us in bondage."[68]

• "We are not ministering merely to the grown person,
but the child yet living in the heart."[69]

The following quotations illustrate how Sandford says a
person may, through visualization techniques travel with Jesus

back through time to heal the inner child:

• "Prayer for the inner child is most effective when vividly pictorial . . . a gift of the Holy Spirit through consecrated imagination. . . ."[70]

• "We have never felt it enough merely to ask that it be done (inner healing). . . . Usually that requires an experiential involvement in some kind of visionary prayer in which we are engaged in the activity with the Lord. . . . Setting a person free from spiritual captivity by (visionary) prayer is one of the most exciting adventures one can have."[71]

• "There is no way to describe how the experience moves from something one could be imagining, having no more reality than pictures in the mind, into an intensely real, emotionally stirring experience."[72]

• "I 'saw' our Lord walking down a steeply sloping dark tunnel. . . . I watched as He walked across a dirty floor. . . . There in a corner, huddled in a fetal position, manacled by wrists and ankles . . . was Jo. She appeared tiny as a child. With His beautiful nail-scarred hands, he deftly gently broke off the shackles. He picked her up, cradling her softly against His chest. I wept for joy and the beauty of it. . . . Then He set her on her feet. . . . As they walked Jo began to grow. . . from a little girl to the grown woman she is. . . . I saw Him turn her loose to frolic in a lovely meadow as He watched, beaming with joy and pride."[73]

The Sandfords And O. Carl Simonton, M. D.:

The Sandfords recommend a plan by Oncologist Simonton in his book, *Getting Well Again.*[74]

• "We place those steps in a parallel column with our references to what the Bible says on the same subject. . . . Christian readers: If cancer regression can be successfully achieved as in this program *without* specific reference to God . . . how much *more* could be accomplished with common sense, medical knowledge, and *prayer*, especially for inner healing which reaches all the way back to those feelings of isolation, neglect and despair the patient experienced in his youth?!"[75]

• Simonton's six week regime includes daily "relaxation and imagery: by end of imagery you are healthy; you see yourself fulfilling life's purpose."[76] Sandford's column of biblical verses contain no verses about relaxation and imagery.[77] The sixth week Simonton says "get in touch with your 'inner guide' (a wise old person within)."[78]

• O. Carl Simonton channels a spirit. He learned how to channel his inner guide from Jose Silva of Silva Mind Control.[79] Anthropologist and shaman Harner says of Simonton's technique of relaxation, visualizing and meeting an inner guide: "This resemblance to the shamanic journey is remarkable."[80] Yet the Sanfords recommend this for Christians: "We have taught all this."[81]

Toronto Blessing:

At a conference held in a church in Coeur d'Alene, Idaho, the Sandfords told of their influence in the "Toronto blessing" because the pastor and counselors in the Toronto Vinyard church go through the Sandfords' training sessions.[82] The Toronto blessing is also known as the laughing ministry where congregations erupt in uncontrollable laughter or weeping, often falling to the floor in ecstatic trances, even barking like dogs or roaring like lions.

John Sandford's Evaluation Of His Ministry:

• "Doctrine is vouchsafed in the Word, but it is not in the Bible; it is the church's historically tested deposit of understanding about the Bible. The Lord reshapes it by revelation."[83]

• "I had been down so many seemingly blind alleys, and suffered so many misleading mystical experiences. . . ."[84]

• "All this drove me to the Scriptures. By then I had been down so many seemingly blind alleys, I wasn't going to have anything if it couldn't be found in the Word of God. . . .

Seeing it in Scripture was not enough. I knew by then I could read into Scripture what I wanted to see. . . . He began to teach me. . . . Though my best way to set people free remains to do it by describing by vision what He does."[85]

• "Visions frequently help in our counseling."[86]

• "Revelation comes again and again in the seeming garb of heresy."[87]

• "We place the cross of Christ between the child and parents back through the generations . . . that all his inheritance be filtered through the cross. This is not magic."[88]

• "America is literally strewn with the wreckage of my mistakes."[89]

Chapter Eighteen:

What Then Shall We Say?

The dust cover of Agnes Sanford's autobiography calls her a free spirit who does not fit a conventional mold. Her books bear this out. Quotations from these books have shown she believed God dwelt in all His creation and Jesus died on the cross to "redeem the unconscious" of men.

During an out of body experience, Sanford received "sealed orders" from Jesus to bring a new Gospel of Healing to this planet. She also commanded God through her prayer of faith—devised during her involvement with New Thought teachers—and healed illness through yoga-like meditation, therapeutic touch, and visualization.

Sanford believed God is energy and she could channel spiritual energy into another person for their healing. She believed we have an actual spiritual body which can travel outside our physical body. This spiritual body is essential to her theology of healing, prayer from a distance, and healing of memories. Healing of the Soul or inner healing was accomplished though going within oneself, instead of "looking to Jesus."

Jesus, our time traveler, literally takes us back through our memories and heals them. He entered the collective unconscious of mankind on the cross. We contact our inner child through visualization or creative imagination with Jesus as our spirit guide. Freudian/Jungian unconscious governs our lives.

Research for this book uncovered some new data on the

development of dynamic psychiatry and how the concept of the subconscious was invented. The origin of the unconscious involved more than Mesmerism and hypnosis. Jung and others used mediums to elucidate the unconscious; Jung used psychotics to develop the archetypes which led to his theory of the collective unconscious. Or we can say he used the abnormal to try to explain the normal. Since the unconscious played an important part in explaining the role of "Jesus" in inner healing/healing of memories and the inner child, one must prayerfully consider whether Christians should be unequally yoked together with non-Christian thought systems which affect our spiritual well being (2 Cor. 6:14). Sanford was bound to Jungian psychology. She was also yoked to anti-Christian New Thought/New Age leaders like Emmett Fox.

We began this book with a discussion of the importance of firm foundations. Our spiritual foundation must be eternally sound. Jesus is our Rock. He is the rock of our salvation (Psalm 95:1). We do not need a questionable "Jesus" who is the product of our imagination to be our spirit guide.

We are like the Israelites who asked for a king because they wanted to be under a system similar to their pagan neighbors. They didn't want to commit to the King of the universe who loved them and had delivered them from bondage. Many Christians today have the same problem as those who lived under the Judges. Instead of seeking God's guidance through knowing His Word, Sanford and her followers who use the inner child and healing of memories are doing what is right in their own eyes. The Prayer of Faith actually bypasses God. Yoga-like meditation and New Age visualization smack of the occult.

The canon of Scripture is closed. We are not to add to God's Word (Deut. 4:2; 12:32; Prov. 30:5-6; Rev. 22:19-19). Sanford based the healing of memories on her claim that God gave her a new gospel of healing.

For centuries Christians never heard of integrating their personalities, pastors never trained in counseling, never looked within "self" to heal their memories. We are to look outward to Jesus who is "the author and finisher of our faith" (Heb. 12:2).

God knows our hearts and our needs. Only He can be our shield and guide. Only He can heal our soul. We need to seek Him, know Him, and believe Him. This comes from studying His attributes and His promises. We need to know His commandments, believe them, and act upon them. He is our reward.

References

Introduction
1 Agnes Sanford, *The Healing Touch of God* (New York, NY: Ballantine Books, 1983) p. 81.
2 Agnes Sanford, *Sealed Orders* (Plainfield, NJ: Logos International, 1972) p. 103

Chapter One: Mother of Inner Healing
1 Sanford, *Sealed Orders*, p. 43.
2 *Ibid.*, p. 43.
3 *Ibid.*, p. 44.
4 *Ibid.*, pp. 75-76.
5 *Ibid.*, pp. 88-89.
6 *Ibid.*, p. 192.
7 *Ibid.*, p. 92.
8 *Ibid.*, p. 241.

Chapter Two: A Free Spirit
1 Sanford, *Sealed Orders*, p. 27.
2 *Ibid.*, p. 23.
3 *Ibid.*.
4 *Ibid.*, p. 27.
5 *Ibid.*, p. 61.
6 *Ibid.*, p. 11.
7 *Ibid.*, p. 23.
8 *Ibid.*, p. 16.
9 *Ibid.*, p. 14.
10 *Ibid.*, p. 99-100.
11 Sanford, *The Healing Light* (New York, NY: Ballantine Books, 1983) p. 12.
12 Sanford, *Sealed Orders*, p. 284.
13 *Ibid.*, pp. 18-19.
14 *Ibid.*, p. 135.
15 Sanford, *Healing Light*, p. 116.
16 Agnes Sanford, *Behold Your God* (St. Paul, MN: Macalester Park Publishing Co., 1959) p. 82.

Chapter Three: Motives for Healing
1 Sanford, *Sealed Orders*, p. 19.
2 *Ibid.*, p. 48.
3 Sanford, *Healing Touch*, p. 40.
4 Sanford, *Sealed Orders*, p. 15.
5 Sanford, *Healing Light*, p. 154.
6 Sanford, *Healing Touch*, p. 44.
7 Sanford, *Sealed Orders*, p. 39.

[8] Sanford, *Healing Touch*, p. 105-106.
[9] *Ibid.*, p. 11.
[10] *Ibid.*, p. 92.
[11] *Ibid.*, p. 93.
[12] *Ibid.*, p. 106.
[13] *Ibid.*, p. 96.
[14] *Ibid.*, p. 100.
[15] *Ibid.*, p. 99.
[16] *Ibid.*, p. 100.
[17] *Ibid.*, p. 102.
[18] *Ibid.*.
[19] Sanford, *Sealed Orders*, pp. 23, 102-103.
[20] Sanford, *Healing Touch*, p. 2.
[21] J. Gresham Machen, *What is Faith?* (Grand Rapids, MI: Eerdmans, 1962) p. 35.
[22] Sanford, *Sealed Orders*, p. 109.
[23] *Ibid.*, p. 59.
[24] *Ibid.*, p. 87.
[25] *Ibid.*, p. 89.
[26] *Ibid.*, p. 101.
[27] *Ibid.*, pp. 107-108.
[28] *Ibid.*, p. 108.
[29] *Ibid.*, p. 94.

Chapter Four: New Thought, New Age, and Agnes

[1] Sanford, *Sealed Orders*, p. 23.
[2] *Ibid.*, pp. 63, 92, 94, 109, 266.
[3] *Ibid.*, p. 281.
[4] *Ibid.*, pp. 281-282.
[5] *Ibid.*, p. 283.
[6] *Ibid.*.
[7] *Ibid.*, p. 295.
[8] Agnes Sanford, *Healing Power of the Bible* (New York, NY: Pillar Books, 1976) p. 210.
[9] Alice Bailey, *Ponder on This* (New York, NY: Lucis, 1983) p. 409.
[10] Sanford, *Sealed Orders*, p. 97.
[11] *Ibid.*, p. 100.
[12] *Ibid.*, p. 106.
[13] *Ibid.*, p. 107.
[14] *Ibid.*.
[15] *Ibid.*, p. 148.
[16] *Ibid.*, p. 103.
[17] *Ibid.*.
[18] Emmett Fox, *The Sermon on the Mount* (New York, NY: Harper & Brothers Publishers, 1938) pp. 2-5.
[19] Emmett Fox, *Life is Consciousness* (Kansas City, MO: Unity School of Christianity, 1940) p. 5.
[20] Fox, *Sermon*, p. 132.
[21] Sanford, *Sealed Orders*, p. 155.
[22] Author Unknown, *Let Your Light Shine* (Unity Village, MO: Unity Books, NA) p. 54.

23 Sanford, *Sealed Orders*, p. 142.

24 *Ibid.*, p. 142.

25 *Ibid.*, p. 148.

26 *Ibid.*, p. 149.

27 Connie Fillmore, *Unity Guide to Healing* (Unity Village, MO: Unity Books, NA) pp. 99-100.

28 *Ibid.*, p. 107.

29 Sanford, *Sealed Orders*, p. 190.

30 Thomas E. Witherspoon, *Myrtle Fillmore Mother of Unity* (Unity Village, MO: Unity Books, 1984) p. 81.

Chapter Five: Agnes and God

1 Agnes Sanford, *Healing Light*, p.18.

2 Agnes Sanford, *Creation Waits* (Plainfield, NJ: Logos, **NA**) p. 7.

3 Sanford, *Sealed Orders*, p.29.

4 *Ibid.*, p.30.

5 Sanford, *Healing Touch of God* (New York, NY: Ballantine Books, 1983) p. 15.

6 Sanford, *Healing Light*, p. 22.

7 Agnes Sanford, *Lost Shepherd* (Plainfield, NJ: Logos, 1971) p. 118.

8 Sanford, *Healing Power*, p. 17.

9 Sanford, *Creation*, p. 8.

10 Sanford, *Healing Power*, p. 75.

11 Sanford, *Healing Touch*, p. 79.

12 Sanford, *Sealed Orders*, p. 117.

13 Sanford, *Creation*, p. 57.

14 Sanford, *Healing Touch,* p. 51.

15 Sanford, *Healing Light*, p. 162.

16 *Ibid.*, pp. 164-165.

Chapter Six: A Blurred Picture of Jesus

1 Sanford, *Sealed Orders*, p. 27.

2 *Ibid.*, p. 52.

3 *Ibid.*, p. 248.

4 Sanford, *Healing Touch*, p. 113.

5 *Ibid.*, pp. 113-114.

6 *Ibid.*, pp. 98-99; 102.

7 *Ibid.*, pp. 107-108.

8 Sanford, *Sealed Orders*, pp. 49, 92, 266, 312.

9 *Ibid* p. 49.

10 Sanford, *Healing Touch*, pp. 125-126.

11 *Ibid.*, p. 126.

12 *Ibid.*, p. 117.

13 Sanford, *Healing Power*, p. 99.

14 *Ibid.*, pp. 25-26.

15 *Ibid.*, p. 26.

16 *Ibid.*, pp. 202-203.

Chapter Seven: Flirting With Spiritism

1 Sanford, *Sealed Orders*, p. 150.

2 *Ibid.*, p. 151.

[3] *Ibid.*, p. 152.

[4] *Ibid.*, p. 153.

[5] *Ibid.*, p. 154.

[6] *Ibid.*, p. 143.

[7] Glen Clark, *God's Reach* (St. Paul, MN: Macalester Park Publishing Co, 1951) p. 54.

[8] *Ibid.*, p. 83.

[9] C. G. Jung, *Modern Man in Search of a Soul* (New York, NY: Harcourt, Brace & World, Inc. A Harvest Book, 1933) p. 173.

[10] Sanford, *Healing Touch*, p. 100.

[11] *Ibid.*, p. 110.

[12] Sanford, *Healing Power*, p. 190.

[13] Sanford, *Healing Gifts of the Spirit* (Philadelphia, PA: J.B. Lippincot, 1966) p. 136.

[14] Sanford, *Sealed Orders*, p. 59.

[15] Sanford, *Healing Power*, p. 178.

[16] Jung, *Modern Man*, p. 206.

[17] H. Brugh Joy, M.D., *Joy's Way* (Los Angeles: J.P. Tarcher, 1979) p. 129.

[18] *Ibid.*, p. 132.

[19] Sanford, *Sealed Orders*, p. 24.

[20] Charles Fillmore, *Mysteries of Genesis* (Kansas City, MO; Unity School of Christianity, 1936) p. 139.

[21] Sanford, *Sealed Orders*, p. 252.

[22] Sanford, *Creation*, p. 46.

[23] C. W. Leadbetter, *Man Visible and Invisible* (Wheaton, IL: The Theosophical Publishing House, 1975) pp. 108-109.

[24] Sanford, *Sealed Orders*, p. 127.

[25] *Ibid.*, pp. 256, 262.

Chapter Eight: Prayer of Faith

[1] Sanford, *Sealed Orders*, p. 284.

[2] Sanford, *Healing Touch*, p. 172.

[3] Sanford, *Sealed Orders*, p. 99.

[4] Sanford, *Healing Power*, p. 9.

[5] Witherspoon, *Myrtle Fillmore*, pp. 121-123.

[6] Sanford, *Healing Touch*, p. 18.

[7] Sanford, *Sealed Orders*, p. 97.

[8] *Ibid.*, p. 102.

[9] *Ibid.*, p. 105.

[10] Sanford, *Healing Gifts*, p. 40.

[11] Sanford, *Healing Touch*, p. 120.

[12] Sanford, *Sealed Orders*, p. 102.

[13] *Ibid.*, p. 103.

[14] *Ibid.*, p. 104.

[15] Sanford, *Healing Power*, p. 17.

[16] *Ibid.*, p. 205.

[17] Sanford, *Healing Touch*, p. 149.

[18] Leadbeater, *Man Visible*, pp. 6-9.

[19] Sanford, *Healing Power*, pp. 17-18.

[20] Ernest Holmes, *The Science of Mind* (New York, NY: Robert M. McBride & Company, 1938) p. 376.

21 Sanford, *Sealed Orders*, p. 104.
22 *Ibid.*, pp. 104-105.
23 *Ibid.*, p. 105.
24 Sanford, *Healing Light*, p. 34.
25 Witherspoon, *Myrtle Fillmore*, p. 38.
26 *Ibid.*, p. 39.
27 Fillmore, *Unity Guide*, pp. 17, 7.

Chapter Nine: Turning God On
1 Sanford, *Healing Light*, pp. 7, 5, 83.
2 Sanford, *Creation*, p. 7.
3 Sanford, *Healing Light*, p. 21.
4 *Ibid.*, p. IX.
5 Fillmore, *Unity Guide*, p. 9.
6 Sanford, *Healing Light*, p. 7.
7 *Ibid.*, p. 22.
8 Sanford, *Healing Touch*, p. 18.
9 *Ibid.*, p. 18.
10 *Ibid.*, p. 19.
11 *Ibid.*, p. 18.
12 *Ibid.*, p. 210.
13 *Drill in Silence* [tract] (Kansas City, MO: Unity School of Christianity, NA) p. 2.
14 Shakti Gawain, *Creative Visualization* (New York, NY: Bantam New Age Books, 1985) p. 4.
15 *Ibid.*, pp. 9-10,16.
16 Sanford, *Sealed Orders*, p. 284.
17 *Ibid.*.
18 Sanford, *Healing Light*, p. 24.
19 Sanford, *Healing Touch*, p. 38.
20 *Ibid.*.
21 *Ibid.*, p. 42.
22 Sanford, *Creation*, pp. 60-61.
23 Fox, *Sermon*, p. 103.
24 Fillmore, *Unity Guide*, pp. 35, 41, 62, 101, 21, 25.
25 Sanford, *Healing Touch*, p. 43.
26 *Ibid.*, p. 50.
27 Sanford, *Healing Light*, p. 7.
28 *Ibid.*, p. 24.
29 Sanford, *Healing Gifts*, p. 57.
30 Fillmore, *Unity Guide*, p. 32.
31 H. Emilie Cady, *Lessons in Truth* (Unity Village, MO: Unity Books, NA) p. 55.
32 Fillmore, *Unity Guide*, p. 79.
33 Gawain, *Creative*, p. 21.
34 *Ibid.*, p. 41.

Chapter Ten: Laying on of Hands
1 Sanford, *Sealed Orders*, p. 108.
2 *Ibid.*, pp. 143, 165.
3 Sanford, *Healing Light*, p. 94.

[4] Sanford, *Sealed Orders*, p. 112.
[5] Sanford, *Healing Light*, p. 18.
[6] Sanford, *Healing Gifts*, p. 66.
[7] Sanford, *Healing Power*, p. 150.
[8] *Ibid.*, p. 91.
[9] *Ibid.*, p. 165.
[10] Sanford, *Healing Gifts*, p. 81.
[11] Sanford, *Healing Light*, p. 81.

Chapter Eleven: Failure of the Prayer of Faith
[1] Sanford, *Sealed Orders*, p. 180.
[2] *Ibid.*, p. 216.
[3] Sanford, *Healing Light*, pp. 150-151.
[4] *Ibid.*, p. 151.
[5] Sanford, *Healing Gifts*, pp. 75-76.
[6] *Ibid.*, p. 76.
[7] *Ibid.*, p. 39.
[8] *Ibid.*, p. 40.
[9] *Ibid.*, p. 41.
[10] Sanford, *Healing Light*, p. 116.
[11] *Ibid.*.
[12] Sanford, *Healing Gifts*, p. 158.
[13] Sanford, *Sealed Orders*, p. 216.
[14] *Ibid.*, p. 218.
[15] *Ibid.*, pp. 134, 218.
[16] *Ibid.*, p. 219.
[17] *Ibid.*, p. 223.
[18] *Ibid.*, p. 225.
[19] Sanford, *Healing Light*, p. 116.
[20] *Ibid.*, p. 117.
[21] *Ibid.*, p. 116.
[22] *Ibid.*, p. 119.
[23] *Ibid.*, p. 132.
[24] Sanford, *Healing Touch*, p. 2.

Chapter Twelve: "Healing of the Soul Never Fails"
[1] Sanford, *Healing Gifts*, p. 10.
[2] *Ibid.*, p. 42.
[3] Sanford, *Sealed Orders*, p. 148.
[4] Sanford, *Healing Touch*, pp. 138-139.
[5] Sanford, *Healing Gifts*, p. 34.
[6] *Ibid.*, p. 120.
[7] Sanford, *Healing Light*, p. 82.
[8] Annie Besant and C. W. Leadbeater, *Thought Forms* (Wheaton, IL: The Theosophical Publishing House, Fourth Quest Book Printing 1980) pp. 36-38.
[9] Sanford, *Healing Gifts*, p. 101.
[10] Besant and Leadbeater, *Thought Forms*, pp. 28, 29.
[11] Sanford, *Healing Touch*, p. 139.
[12] Besant and Leadbeater, *Thought Forms*, back cover.
[13] Sanford, *Healing Light*, p. 55.

[14] Sanford, *Healing Touch*, p. 139.
[15] Sanford, *Creation*, p. 143.
[16] Sanford, *Healing Touch*, p. 139.
[17] Sanford, *Healing Gifts*, pp. 174-175.
[18] *Ibid.*, p. 136.
[19] Sanford, *Healing Touch*, p. 139.
[20] Sanford, *Healing Gifts*, p. 137.

Chapter Thirteen: Inner Healing and Memories
[1] Sanford, *Healing Gifts*, p. 42.
[2] *Ibid.*, pp. 42, 123.
[3] Chafer and Walvoord, *Major Bible Themes* (Grand Rapids, MI: Zondervan, 1976) p. 206.
[4] *Ibid.*, pp. 208, 209.
[5] Sanford, *Sealed Orders*, p. 189.
[6] Fox, *Sermon*, p. 45.
[7] Sanford, *Sealed Orders*, p. 103.
[8] *Ibid.*, p. 266.
[9] Jung, *Modern*, p. 31.
[10] Sanford, *Healing Light*, p. 116.
[11] Sanford, *Sealed Orders*, p. 191.
[12] Sanford, *Creation*, p. 36; *Sealed Orders*, p. 191.
[13] Sanford, Healing Light, p. 158.
[14] Sanford, *Healing Gifts*, pp. 108, 116; *Healing Touch*, pp. 72-75; *Sealed Orders*, pp. 195-196.
[15] Sanford, *Healing Touch*, p. 74.
[16] Sanford, *Sealed Orders*, p. 103.
[17] Sanford, *Healing Gifts*, p. 125.
[18] *Ibid.*, p. 119.
[19] *Ibid.*, pp. 121-122.
[20] *Ibid.*, p. 150.
[21] *Ibid.*, p. 141.
[22] *Ibid.*, p. 137.
[23] Sanford, *Healing Touch*, p. 120.
[24] Sanford, *Healing Gifts*, p. 152.
[25] *Ibid.*, p. 152.

Chapter Fourteen: The Inner Child
[1] Jeremiah Abrams, *Reclaiming the Inner Child* (Los Angeles: Jeremy P. Tarcher, Inc., 1990) p. 6.
[2] Jung, *Modern*, p. 228.
[3] Henri F. Ellenberger, *The Discovery of the Unconscious: The History and Evolution of Dynamic Psychiatry* (New York, NY: Basic Books, 1970) p. 661.
[4] *Ibid.*, p. 662.
[5] *Ibid.*, p. 665.
[6] *Ibid.*, p. 667.
[7] Sanford, *Healing Gifts*, p. 165-166.
[8] J. I. Packer, *Knowing God* (Downers Grove, IL: InterVarsity Press, 1973) p. 41.
[9] *Ibid.*, 41.
[10] *Ibid.*.

[11] *Ibid.*, p. 43.

[12] *Ibid.*, p. 44.

[13] Bernie Siegal, *Love, Medicine and Miracles* (New York, NY: Harper Perennial, 1990) p. 148.

[14] Jeremiah Abrams, ed., *Reclaiming the Inner Child* (Los Angeles, CA: Jeremy P. Tarcher, Inc., 1990) p. 293.

[15] Sanford, *Healing Power*, pp. 75, 71.

[16] C. G. Jung, *Reclaiming*, p. 29.

[17] Sanford, *Healing Gifts*, p. 122.

[18] Abrams, *Reclaiming*, p. 34.

[19] *Ibid.*, pp. 242.

Chapter Fifteen: The Source of the Unconscious

[1] Lancelot Law Whyte, *The Unconscious Before Freud* (New York, NY: Social Science Paperbacks, 1967) p. 9.

[2] *Ibid.*, p. 175.

[3] Ellenberger, *Discovery*, Intro. p. VI.

[4] *Ibid.*, p. 85.

[5] *Ibid.*, pp. 120-121.

[6] *Ibid.*, Intro. p. VI.

[7] *Ibid.*, pp. 117-119.

[8] *Ibid.*, p. 671.

[9] *Ibid.*, p. 675.

[10] *Ibid.*, p. 666.

[11] *Ibid.*, p. 689.

[12] *Ibid.*, p. 671.

[13] Michael Harner, *The Way of the Shaman* (New York: Bantam Books, 1982) pp. 89-108.

[14] Ellenberger, *Discovery*, p. 671.

[15] Morton Kelsey, *Psychology, Medicine and Christian Healing* (San Francisco, CA: Harper and Row, 1988) p. 258.

[16] Ellenberger, *Discovery*, p. 890.

[17] Brown, *Freud and Post-Freudians* (Baltimore, MD: Penguin Books, 1971) p. 44.

Chapter Sixteen: The Collective Unconscious

[1] Holmes, *Science*, p. 347.

[2] Sanford, *Healing Light*, p. 121.

[3] Sanford, *Healing Touch*, pp. 97-99.

[4] Sanford, *Healing Gifts*, pp. 160, 136.

[5] Sanford, *Healing Touch*, p. 99.

[6] *Ibid.*, pp. 83-84.

[7] *Ibid.*, p. 72.

[8] *Ibid.*, p. 64.

[9] Sanford, *Healing Power,* p. 26.

[10] Sanford, *Healing Touch,* pp. 202-203.

[11] Sanford, *Creation*, pp. 105-106.

[12] Sanford, *Sealed Orders*, p. 312.

[13] Sanford, *Creation*, p. 72.

[14] Sanford, *Healing Power*, p. 40.

[15] *Ibid.*, p. 41.

[16] Sanford, *Sealed Orders*, p. 233.
[17] *Ibid.*, p. 291.
[18] *Ibid.*, p. 307; *Creation*, p. 3.
[19] *Ibid.*, p. 15.
[20] Fox, *Sermon*, p. 14.
[21] Sanford, *Healing Power*, pp. 34, 41, 49.
[22] *Ibid.*, pp. 49-51.
[23] Sanford, *Healing Gifts*, p. 173.
[24] J. Allan Hobson, *The Dreaming Brain*, as quoted by Lynne Lamberg in *American Health* magazine, July 1987.

Chapter Seventeen: Agnes's Ministry: The Ministry of John Sandford
[1] John & Paula Sandford, *The Transformation of the Inner Man* (South Plainfield, N.J.: Bridge Publishing, Inc. 1982) p. vi.
[2] John and Paula Sandford, *Healing of the Wounded Spirit* (Tulsa, OK: Victory House, 1985) p. 316.
[3] *Ibid.*, p. 255.
[4] Sanford, *Transformation*, p. 309.
[5] *Ibid.*, p. 157.
[6] Sanford, *Wounded Spirit*, p. 329
[7] *Ibid.*, p. 329.
[8] *Ibid.*, p. 329.
[9] *Ibid.*, p. 18.
[10] John and Paula Sandford, *The Elijah Task* (Plainfield N.J.: Logos International, 1977) p. 13.
[11] *Ibid.*, p. 136.
[12] *Ibid.*, p. 137.
[13] Sanford, *Wounded Spirit*, p. 435.
[14] Sanford, *Elijah*, p. 138.
[15] *Ibid.*, p. 135.
[16] Sanford, *Wounded Spirit*, pp. 224-225.
[17] *Ibid.*, p. 225.
[18] Sanford, *Transformation*, p. 72.
[19] Sanford, *Wounded Spirit*, p. 405.
[20] Sanford, *Elijah*, p. 125.
[21] Sanford, *Wounded Spirit*, p. 406.
[22] Sanford, *Transformation*, p. 127.
[23] *Ibid.*, pp. 5, 82, 227, 295-315, 313, 329; Sanford, *Wounded Spirit*, pp. 64, 237, 414; Sanford, *Elijah*, p. 221.
[24] Sanford, *Elijah*, p. 302.
[25] *Ibid.*, p. 125.
[26] *Ibid.*, p. 134.
[27] Sanford, *Wounded Spirit*, p. 93.
[28] Sanford, *Elijah*, p. 132.
[29] *Ibid.*, p. 228.
[30] Sanford, *Wounded Spirit*, p. 97.
[31] Sanford, *Transformation*, pp. 278-279.
[32] *Ibid.*, p. 62.
[33] Sanford, *Elijah*, p. 204.
[34] Sanford, *Wounded Spirit*, p. 377.
[35] Sanford, *Elijah*, p. 206.

[36] *Ibid.*, p. 33.
[37] Sandford, *Transformation*, p. 82.
[38] *Ibid.*, p. 197.
[30] *Ibid.*, p. 81.
[40] Sandford, *Wounded Spirit*, p. 111.
[41] Sandford, *Elijah*, p. 189.
[42] *Ibid.*, pp. 180-181.
[43] Sandford, *Wounded Spirit*, p. 286.
[44] Michael Harner, *The Way of the Shaman* (New York: Bantam New Age Books, 1982) p. 177.
[45] Sandford, *Wounded Spirit*, p. 148.
[46] *Ibid.*, pp. 149-150.
[47] Sandford, *Elijah*, p. 182.
[48] Sandford, *Wounded Spirit*, pp. 12-13.
[49] *Ibid.*, p. 12.
[50] *Ibid.*, p. 11.
[51] *Ibid.*, p. 112.
[52] *Ibid.*, p. 388.
[53] *Ibid.*, p. 389.
[54] Sandford, *Transformation*, p. 212.
[55] *Ibid.*, p. 216.
[56] *Ibid..*
[57] *Ibid.*, p. 26.
[58] Sandford, *Wounded Spirit*, p. 17.
[59] These topics are taken from chapters in Sandford, *Transformation*, and Sandford, *Wounded Spirit.*
[60] Sandford, *Wounded Spirit*, pp. 337-338.
[61] *Ibid.*, p. XX.
[62] *Ibid.*, p. 46.
[63] Sandford, *Transformation*, pp. 253-254.
[64] Sandford, *Wounded Spirit*, p. 151.
[65] *Ibid.*, p. 9.
[66] *Ibid.*, p. 11.
[67] *Ibid.*, p. 112.
[68] *Ibid.*, p. 59.
[69] Sandford, *Transformation*, p. 102.
[70] *Ibid.*, p. 146.
[71] Sandford, *Wounded Spirit*, p. 157.
[72] *Ibid.*, p. 157.
[73] *Ibid.*, pp. 149-150.
[74] *Ibid.*, p. 436.
[75] *Ibid..*
[76] *Ibid.*, p. 439.
[77] *Ibid..*
[78] *Ibid.*, p. 440.
[79] Jose Silva, *The Silva Mind Control Method* (New York: Pocket Books, Simon & Schuster, 1977) p. 79.
[80] Harner, *Shaman*, pp. 176-177.
[81] Sandford, *Wounded Spirit*, p. 441.
[82] Personal Communication.
[83] Sandford, *Elijah*, p. 167.

[84] Sandford, *Wounded Spirit*, p. 413.

[85] *Ibid.*, pp. 151-153.

[86] Sandford, *Elijah*, p. 196.

[87] *Ibid.*, p. 152.

[88] Sandford, *Wounded Spirit*, p. 47.

[89] Sandford, *Elijah*, p. 69.